SEYI FALAIYE

the Father's Heart

**THE TYPE OF FATHER THAT YOU CHOOSE
TO BE IS THE LEGACY YOU CHOOSE TO LEAVE**

Copyright © 2021 Seyi Falaiye

All rights reserved under International Copyright Laws. No part of this book may be reproduced or transmitted, downloaded, or stored in or introduced into any information storage and retrieval system in any form without the written permission of the Publisher and/or the Author.

ISBN: 978-1-7368215-1-0 (Printed)
ISBN: 978-1-7368215-2-7 (EBook)

Published 2021.

Library of Congress Control Number: 2021908905

Cover Design & Layout by: Kingdom Branding

Printed in the United States of America

DEDICATION

This book is dedicated to God the Father, the ultimate example of fatherhood. To my father, who was a big inspiration for this book and to the many current and future fathers around the world. Fatherhood is a challenging but very rewarding blessing that comes from the Lord. It is a very serious responsibility; therefore, this dedication goes to the fathers who are making an effort to leave a legacy for their children and grandchildren. This book is also for the fathers who need to start making an effort—be encouraged and remember that it is never too late to start a lasting legacy.

All praise and thanks go, exclusively, to the Lord Jesus Christ for providing this opportunity to share my insight, my life, and the lessons learned from his precious word to help men become the fathers and leaders they are called to be.

Additional thanks go to my brother Rotimi Kehinde, Kingdom Branding, and GodKulture Global for his support, friendship, and effort in getting this book into the hands of fathers from every walk of life. God's blessing be abundantly upon you.

A final thanks goes to my family for sticking together through the thick and the thin. May God bless you all richly and bountifully.

In all things, may God receive the glory.

FOREWORD

I am so excited that my friend, Seyi, has written a book on Fatherhood. Fatherhood is the missing piece in today's society. We live in an ever-changing world but the principle and concept of fatherhood remains invaluable. Fatherhood.org states that children that grow up in father-absent homes are more likely to suffer emotional and behavioral problems among other issues. This is a crisis. In 2017, The Census Bureau data showed that one in four children were living without a father in the home. Our ignorance or lack of appropriate attention to this issue is feeding this monster. That's why this book is so relevant and timely.

My father taught me a lot of things, like the value in having a good name. I'll never forget the places and spaces I found myself in, more times than not, the individuals always knew my father. They would go on and on about how amazing my father was. I can't even imagine my upbringing without my father. His calm demeanor, his creativity in songwriting, his humility and grace with which he approached life and his decision making have made my siblings and I the leaders that we are today.

There is no replacement for the evenings he would teach my brothers and I math; or drive me to my special lesson to prepare for my exams. My father raised us to be visionaries and creatives. He taught us about prayer, the Bible, and disciplined us when necessary. The virtues that have become part of my core values come from the principles that I've watched him exhibit over the years.

Some are:

- An unreserved love for his wife and children
- A pursuit of faith and spiritual growth
- Fairness and justice in dealing with conflict
- A commitment to facilitating quality education for his children
- An unwavering passion for music and creative arts
- A sense of humor and wit

You see, Fatherhood is about leadership. Fathers are leaders and they set the tone of leadership development in the home. Fatherhood is about guidance. They provide vision and direction. It is about sacrifice and selfless love. True fathers want their children to do better than them. Fatherhood is about legacy.

Seyi has masterfully written a timeless material that is more than a book. It is a roadmap for anyone who seeks to understand the power that fathers wield. It is a rallying call to action. The Father's Heart will transform your thinking and is highly recommended because it is definitely a game-changer.

Rotimi Kehinde
Founder/President
GodKulture Global

TABLE OF CONTENTS

Introduction xi

Part One: What is Fatherhood? 13

    What is Fatherhood? 15

    The Place of Fathers in Today's Society 19

    The Importance of Fatherhood 23

    The Spiritual Importance of Fatherhood 27

Part Two: The Collapse of Fatherhood 33

    The Breakdown of Fatherhood 35

    The Irresponsible Father 37

    The Unaccountable Father 41

    The Absentee Father 45

    The Dishonorable Father 63

    The Domineering Father 67

    The Abusive Father 81

    The Passive Father 97

Part Three: Do Your Fatherly Duty 103

    The Duties of a Father 105

    Protector 107

    Provider 113

    Guide 117

Part Four: Are You Fulfilling Your Responsibility?......123

    The Responsibilities of a Father......125

    Nurture......127

    Success, Gratitude, and Humility......131

    Honesty and Availability......137

    Setting (or Resetting) a Legacy......143

Part Five: The True Heart of the Father......149

    The True Heart of the Father......151

    Holiness......153

    Love and Sacrifice......157

    Discipline and Protection......161

    Provider and Guide......165

References......175

INTRODUCTION

The battle for the family is very real and very intense. The battle for fathers and genuine fatherhood, especially, is real on the physical and spiritual forefront of societies around the world. In our world today, the value and the significance of fathers in the home is sinking and the family is paying the price whether they know it or not.

First and foremost, in all things, it is important to give credit and respect where it is due and when it comes to matters of fatherhood, there is no exception. In the world and throughout history there have been some very remarkable men who have been dedicated and active in the rearing of their children and, sometimes, the children of other men. To each and every one of those men, may God bless you and continue to give you wisdom and grace to continue the good work that you are doing. Just as much as a mother, a father who is active in the life of his children is a blessing to them, not just for the present but for years to come.

For those who will read this book, the ultimate purpose is not to demean the men in the world who are fulfilling their calling of being a good father and taking care of their wives and children. This book is also not meant to undermine or demean the work that so many married and single mothers, aunts, and grandmothers put into their children and grandchildren in raising them with priceless values and standards in order to be productive members of society. To the contrary, this book is meant to address the issues within fatherhood—with the intent to bring awareness and positive change to this thing we call being a father.

This book serves to encourage all men to step up, step forward, and be the father that God has created us to be. As we lean into God's way of fatherhood, we will begin to improve the legacies we leave for our children to follow. Along with our wife and children, we will be able to live according to His values, attitude, and doctrines through the Holy Spirit when we wholeheartedly take on fatherhood.

I pray that as you read this book, you allow God to speak to your heart. Permit Him to point you in the right direction. Allow God to show you where you need improvement, he will lead you, he will not desert you. May God bless you through this book. I pray that you may learn to grow an honorable legacy as a man and father.

Part One:

WHAT IS FATHERHOOD?

Part One: What is Fatherhood?

WHAT IS FATHERHOOD?

—

Our world is constantly changing, evolving, growing, and ever looking to redefine things in society, such as political correctness, gender relations, religion, and other issues including what it means to be a man and the definition of fatherhood. As I sit and reflect on the true definition and significance of fatherhood, I sometimes wonder what that word truly means and how it fits in our world today. This book is not meant to diminish the roles of mothers who are equal and an integral part of the family structure. However, it is a call to men as a reminder that God has called each and every one of us to be the head of his household. To put it plainly, as a father, you are needed. You are called to lead your family in the will and the way of the Lord and you have been appointed as the spiritual covering over your family. Will you answer the call or leave your duty to the charge of others? Regrettably, some men choose the latter, leaving mothers, relatives, the government, and others in society to gather the pieces left behind in their absence. In light of this reality the question still remains. What is the true definition of a father?

According to Webster's Dictionary, a father is defined as: "A male parent or a man who exercises paternal care over other persons; paternal protector or a provider." There are several key words I would like to touch on as far as the definition of a father goes. First, the individual is a male who actively parents. He is not just a person who shares the DNA of a child. This means that this book is directed not just to biological fathers. It speaks to the stepfathers, the grandfathers, the foster fathers, and any other male who has the charge of taking care of children. The second part is that he provides paternal care, paternal protection, and paternal provision. These responsibilities should not be passed to any other individual with the exception of death, incapacitation, or invalidity. More importantly, it is paramount for all men to understand that fatherhood is not just a passing phase in life. Once a man becomes a father that charge is given until the day that he dies. It is important to know that every father's legacy, for better or worse, lives on in the lives of his children and other generations to come. With such a responsibility and with such consequences, the magnitude of true fatherhood should not be taken lightly but should be seen as a privilege and an honor that each man should bear with pride and gratitude to God.

I have two boys who according to the doctors were never supposed to be born, because of conditions that would make it hard for my wife and I to have children. This, understandably, was hard news to take when we heard it but we kept praying and a year or two later our first son was born and two and a half years later we were blessed with our second. Despite the medical prognosis given to us, God saw otherwise and blessed us with two boys who I am proud to be a father to. I am by no means a perfect father and I still have a lot to learn but every day when I look in their faces and see their smiles, hear their laughter, and even comfort their tears, I can only thank God for His mercy and praise Him for showing that He, not the doctors, has the last word. In addition, it allows me to do whatever I need to do to make sure that they are protected, provided for, and raised to eventually grow to be the men that God has created them to be. I realize the blessing that God has given to me and I take the raising of my sons seriously and so should every man who has been blessed with children. There is no better or greater charge that can be entrusted to a man.

Part One: What is Fatherhood?

THE PLACE OF FATHERS IN TODAY'S SOCIETY

—

A father is to have a good work-home balance as best as his capacity is to do so. Historically, one measure of manhood has been for the man to go out and work to provide for his wife and children and while this is still true, a father is also needed at home to help raise his children. This responsibility is not solely a woman's job and regardless of cultural norms it takes both a mother and a father to fulfill their roles in the home. I have truly come to the conclusion that it takes a man to raise a boy who will one day, be a man himself. Afterall, only a man can teach a boy how to be a man. As great, important, and respectable a mother is and as much influence as a mother may have, as a woman, she cannot fully teach a boy what it truly means to be a man. God designed for the family to have a father and a mother for this very reason.

The reality however is that not every family is structured the way God intended it to be. For cases in which one or both parents are unavailable, the family must place their trust in the Lord and navigate with wisdom, patience, and assurance that God will not leave you or desert you in your affliction. While this is often easier said than done, it is possible to make something out of a seemingly dire situation and there are many people who can attest to this. On the other hand, for those who have both parents, the place of a father should be in the home as much as possible and effectively in the life of each one of his children. Even in cases of divorce or separation, a father must be present as much as the law and his parental rights will allow. There can be no substitute for the fulfillment of this responsibility and even in this broken society a father can still fulfill his calling if he truly aspires to do so. Society cannot determine how much a father you are- you do.

As the evolution of values and priorities in our culture develops, it is easy to see the methodical descent in society's view of fatherhood and its place amongst us. An individual does not have to look very far to see this issue, since it can be seen wherever we look. This can be seen in the lives of people around us as well as its increasingly prominent portrayal in the media. In the entertainment industry, fathers are often given the image of an irresponsible, uninformed, immature, or ultimately failing individual who often tends to serve as a beacon of indifference and disappointment. While it can sometimes appear to be humorous and somewhat entertaining to watch, it is a manifestation of a deeper problem—the displacement of fathers and the perceived need for them in today's society.

Over the years, there are several single mothers that I have had the privilege of calling my friends over the course of my life. They usually tend to share some of their struggles and victories in life as they work to raise their kids, but in more than a few of these ladies' lives, one thing that they share is the fact that the fathers of their children tend to be unreliable, untrustworthy, or simply nowhere to be found. For one of these young ladies, her daughter now calls her father by his first name and treats him like any other man on the street because he has neglected to be a regular part of her life. Another confessed that she, after many attempts to give him the chance at being a regular part of his children's lives, has all but given up hope and trust in him. As a result, she is very hesitant to even leave their children with him even though she works multiple jobs to support her family. These are just some of the stories that seem to have become commonplace in our world today and this simply should not be. God did not design this to be the case but in this broken world there are fathers that tend to fail to live up to their calling.

Occurrences like these have inevitably led to a shift in society in which we have children who grow up angry, disappointed, and hurt by the very men who are charged with their safety, upbringing, and nurture. We are left with children who are confused, feel rejected and unwanted, and struggle more with finding direction when there is no father in the home or active in their lives. We, as fathers, need to make sure that we are fulfilling our call to being a true father to our children. We need to make sure that we are caring, protecting, and providing for our children. To do any less is to be a failure in our responsibilities and it is something each man will ultimately be accountable to God for at the end of his life. Whether you believe it or not, every man will give an account to God not just for his own life but also for what happens to his family. Make the best of the opportunity you have today and remember that a legacy can always be changed for better or worse—let us aim for a better legacy than yesterday.

Part One: What is Fatherhood?

THE IMPORTANCE OF FATHERHOOD

—

There is no measure of value that can be put on having a good father in the home. Fathers are extremely important to the growth and well-being of children in every society. This is not to discount the effort that women, especially single mothers, put into the family. The effort they put in is invaluable and cannot easily be replaced however, God designed the family to have a father and a mother for a specific reason. A reason that is rapidly eroding in today's world. A father serves in several functions that will be discussed later in this book but for now let us focus on how important it is to take fatherhood as seriously as God the Father does.

It is crucial to note that fatherhood has more than just a physical aspect to it. There is an equally important and ever-present spiritual component to being a father. Fatherhood is so important that even the Lord Jesus, while living on earth never faltered in His spiritual relationship with God the Father as is documented throughout the Gospels. Even still today, when we pray, Jesus intercedes on our behalf to God the Father. It is interesting to note that, in addition to God the Father,

Jesus showed the importance of a physical father in the home through Joseph, His non-biological father who raised him from his birth alongside Mary, Jesus' mother. He demonstrated the spiritual side as He spoke frequently and consistently to God the Father during His years of ministry, His time in the Garden of Gethsemane, and even up to the time of his crucifixion. During the time Jesus was on the Earth, the Father shared His heart with the Son so that the ultimate redemption of mankind could be completed all the while teaching us the way that we should live and enjoy all that He has for us along the way.

CHILDREN OFTEN LOOK AT THEIR FATHERS AND CAN ATTRIBUTE THE CHARACTERISTICS THEY SEE AS WELL AS THE SUCCESSES AND FAILURES OF THEIR FATHERS TO WHAT GOD IS LIKE.

In the years of Jesus' ministry, His sole purpose was to do the will of God the Father and to do this effectively, Jesus spent a lot of time in prayer. It is important to see that God the Father did not send Jesus and leave Him alone. Rather, He communed with Jesus regularly and even made sure that Jesus had Joseph as an earthly father figure. In John 14:6, Jesus stated, "I am the way, the truth, and the life. No man comes to the Father but by me." This verse demonstrates the closeness of the Father and the Son. The only way to the Father is through the Son. This would not be possible if there was a disconnect between the Father and the Son. As fathers, we must never forget or underestimate our importance and we should always aspire to a close and unbroken relationship with all of our children. This delights the Lord.

As I watch my sons grow, I love to be around them even on the days where they are extra active or not having their best day. One of the most anticipated times of my day is picking them up from the school bus, all because I like to see them and spend time with them. If I can be like this with my children as an imperfect man and father, I can only imagine how God feels about us and how He feels about fatherhood overall. Spending quality time with our children is paramount and it emulates the great importance that Jesus placed on being in communion with the Father. The relationship between Jesus and the Father was so intimate that on the cross when the Father could not look upon the sin Jesus had taken on Jesus could feel the loss of the Father's presence. In Matthew 26:47, the scripture states, "And about the ninth hour Jesus cried with a loud voice, saying, Eli, Eli, lama sabachthani? that is, My God, my God, why hast thou forsaken me?" During this time, the union between father and son was utterly broken and both the Father and the Son were temporarily separated from one another- and they could both feel it. While this relationship was on a grand spiritual scale, it demonstrated the closeness in relationship that a father needs to have with his children. In order for a good relationship between a father and his children to blossom, good and constant communion needs to be prioritized.

As a father, one essential way I have learned to build such a relationship is to remember and understand that being a father, despite what the world may say, is a blessing from God and not a burden. When a father sees his children as a blessing, he will want to spend as much time enjoying his blessing as possible. In watching my children grow, I realize more and more how much they have blessed my life and as much as I sometimes can grow physically weary from the workday and may need some time to myself to recharge,

I could not see myself without them. I love to be around them and I love when they want to share their stories and their frustrations, their ups and their downs. Each moment is precious and invaluable and as I commune with my children, I want to be there as they grow and have the chance to share in their lives. Spending time with them is of the utmost importance to setting a legacy that will live on in their lives forever.

Part One: What is Fatherhood?

THE SPIRITUAL IMPORTANCE OF FATHERHOOD

—

God has called every father to be the spiritual head of his household. By being physically or spiritually absent, a father violates this God-given ordinance. Amongst church-going families in homes with two parents, sixty percent of church attendees are women. We are living in a time where mothers are the ones doing the praying, taking the children to church, teaching them about the Lord, and volunteering in ministry. Ultimately, many children are learning about the Lord primarily from their mothers when the Lord has explicitly called fathers to spearhead this responsibility. We are the spiritual covering over our families but many of us fail to live up to this and we leave our families exposed in pursuit of other things.

When a man chooses something else over attending church, or leading his family in following the Bible, the lesson that the children learn is that there are other priorities that come first. Whether that priority is watching sports, working and making money, or sleeping in, it is made clear to the children that church is of secondary importance.

More times than not, when a father demonstrates that his spiritual life is not his main priority his children will often follow suit and the little girl then becomes a young woman who begins to pursue men like her father—men who do not love or look to pursue a relationship with the Lord and the boys become men who follow in the footsteps of the legacy set by their father. In this way, a cycle begins and the children and upcoming generations drift further and further away from a walk with the Lord.

It is important to take note that, while we are responsible and accountable for our own actions as individuals, fathers are accountable to God for the decisions they make in the upbringing of their families. In 1 Samuel 2-4, the Bible speaks about such a case involving the High Priest, Eli, and his two sons Hophni and Phinehas. The sons of Eli, who were lacking in proper upbringing by their father, ultimately crossed the line with their disrespect and complacency with the things of God and their holy duties as priests. Eventually God decided to take action. In one day, God removed them from their positions as priests and wiped them all out. In this case, while Eli was not responsible for the specific decisions and actions of his children it is not far from reality to believe that their rebellion did not begin overnight and the Bible makes no mention of any attempt by Eli to correct or discipline his children. By his failure to correct his children, Eli became complicit in their lack of respect for what they did as priests and they all paid the price for their actions. Imagine what could have been if Eli had taken his responsibilities as a father seriously. What could have been if he had held his children to account whenever they shirked or abused their priestly callings?

As Eli failed to correct his sons, there are many fathers in our world today who, if they are even present in the home, have a tendency in leaving the disciplining of their children to others. The reasons range from laziness to inexperience to a need or desire to be friends with their children in order to be seen as the cool parent but regardless of the motive, the structure that children need is significantly less or nonexistent. While we are not to be harsh with correcting our children, we are to be firm and loving in our chosen methods of correcting them. This ensures that we follow the lesson given by King Solomon in the book of Proverbs where he states "Train up a child in the way that he should go and when he is old, he will not depart from it" (Proverbs. 22:6). This is a message that it is your responsibility to raise your children. Do not leave it to others and do not neglect your calling. It may not always be easy but it is always worth it because a legacy can build or destroy a family for generations to come.

WE ARE TO BE FIRM BUT LOVING IN THE CORRECTION OF OUR CHILDREN. WITHOUT LOVE THEY CAN EVENTUALLY BECOME BROKEN PEOPLE.

A much deeper and more serious aspect to the spiritual importance of fatherhood is one that is often not spoken about and one that some do not even believe exists. This is the fact that we have a powerful and unseen enemy who lurks in the shadows and strikes methodically and with deadly precision. He is known as Satan the opposer and the accuser of men; he is a fallen angel who was cast out of Heaven for his failed attempt to usurp the throne of God and, while cast down and ultimately defeated by the sacrifice of Jesus on the cross, he continues to try to work against the sovereignty of God's holiness. Satan hates God and everything that He stands for especially when it comes to the family.

Since the beginning, Satan has looked to destroy families in an attempt to foil that which God has deemed to be good and wholesome. God Himself has a family which is made up of each and every person who has accepted Jesus Christ as Lord and Savior through the sacrificial work of the cross. He cherishes each and every individual regardless of race, color, gender, financial status, or anything else. He welcomes all who look to join His family, and He calls to everyone to be a part of His family simply because of His fatherly love for each and every one of us who He created. God is a father with no preference.

Satan hates that God has a family and one of his main plans is to try to hurt God by damaging and devastating something near and dear to the heart of God. His main plan has been to take fathers out of the picture and he has had some success in his mission. His plan is simple, since he cannot defeat God, fathers are his next target. Remove the head from the rest of the family and it cannot operate as it should. It is a trap that, while straightforward, is very effective due to our fallen nature. Men have failed their families ever since Adam and Eve were in the Garden of Eden when Eve was deceived by the serpent and ate of the fruit that God had forbidden them to eat. Adam, a bystander, who should have intervened and defended Eve against the deception of the serpent, proceeded to partake in eating the fruit. He then proceeded to blame God for giving him Eve in an attempt to excuse his sin. In this action, Adam failed Eve and took no responsibility for his failure.

Although Eve received her own punishment for giving in to temptation, Adam was not spared for not fulfilling his calling in being the leader he was supposed to be. Like Eli's story, Eve was punished for her own decision while Adam was punished for his complacency in fulfilling his role as head of the family. God does not take this charge lightly and neither should we. Being a father is not just a passing on of genetics, it is the passing on of a legacy that Satan looks to destroy.

Throughout history, the devil has taken aim at making an underestimation of the importance of a father in the home and in society. He has worked at removing and unsettling fathers and fatherhood in order to disrupt the family, leaving homes in disorder often followed by a trail of pain, anger, and hurt. Note that while each man has different vices and weaknesses, we have an enemy who is cunning and exploits those weaknesses to the detriment of fulfilling our calling to lead, protect, provide, and care for our families. We need to make sure that we are combating the enemy's plans to foil our success by doing our due diligence towards our children. The Apostle Paul urges fathers in the scriptures when he states, "But if anyone does not provide for his own family, especially for his own household, he has denied the faith and is worse than an unbeliever" (1 Timothy 5:8). The devil smiles when we choose to pursue our own desires over the needs of our families. We must return to the duty that God has given to us and we must glorify God by fulfilling His plan and purpose, by being good fathers and husbands and leaving a godly path and legacy for future generations to follow.

To those who may not know Jesus Christ and to those who may disagree with Christianity, this book still stands with God's initiative that an active father in the home is an invaluable blessing given by God. When a child has a father in the home it can function to the betterment of the child and work towards allowing the father to play the role that he was created for. Again, this does not diminish the role of mothers, especially single mothers, but fathers were created to lead their families and thus should fulfill their callings. Alas, many do not and the mothers and the children often pay the price. This is not the will of God.

His will is that all men will rise up and lead their families to the best of their abilities in serving the Lord. Fathers, despite what society, Hollywood, and the devil may say, you are important, you are needed, and you are valued. It is time to step up to the plate and be exactly what you were called to be: visible, active, and involved.

REVIEW & ANALYSIS

Take some time to review this section. Whether you are by yourself or in a group, be honest with yourself about the following questions:

- What is fatherhood to you?
- As a father (or father to be) how do you view the role of a father?
- In your opinion, what characteristics define the ideal father?
- How do you feel about today's views of fatherhood in society?
- What are your views on the importance of fatherhood?
- How important do you feel it is to have a present father in the lives of his children? Why?
- Do you believe that every father, present or not, leaves a legacy? Why or why not?

Part Two:

THE COLLAPSE OF FATHERHOOD?

Part Two: The Collapse of Fatherhood

THE BREAKDOWN OF FATHERHOOD

—

As I mentioned previously, fatherhood has never been easy and it has always required sacrifice in one area or another, but it is also one of the biggest blessings and responsibilities a man could ever hope to have. As times have changed, the mindset of many has changed towards their children and their role as a father with many now seeing it as a stumbling block to self-fulfillment and fully enjoying life or achieving career goals. I have seen and heard many men who murmur and nitpick about their children and the ways that their children have brought disruption to their lives. While it is true that children certainly bring their own individual challenges and changes, when I hear such chatter, I just shake my head and can't help but feel sorry for them and their children. With the increasing requirements of society and the distractions of our ever-evolving civilization, fatherhood is changing and this chapter will go into the various issues that fathers face and some of the traps they fall into. As you read, you may find out that you fall into one of these categories and don't even know it. Being made aware of the shortcomings and traps that fathers fall into is the first step to refining your legacy and learning to follow the Father's heart.

Part Two: The Collapse of Fatherhood

THE IRRESPONSIBLE FATHER

—

There have always been people in the world who live irresponsible and reckless lifestyles and this can easily spill over into the arena of parenthood. By definition, an irresponsible person is an individual who cannot or does not answer to a higher authority or cannot based on age or circumstance. An irresponsible person is also someone who chooses not to be accountable for their actions due to a lack of a sense of responsibility. In many cases, when a father is irresponsible, he may not see how it may affect his wife and children and, even worse, he may not care. In general, many children tend to look to their fathers for guidance and direction but when we as fathers fail to be responsible, we enter a dangerous arena. Our children have a tendency to, consciously or unconsciously, equate our failures to what God must be like. The mindset turns into a matter of "If God is anything like my father, I cannot trust God either" because the distrust and disappointment tends to echo. It is important to mention that God is love. He loves every one of us and He does not like to be misrepresented by the way we treat our children when it leaves them hurt, angry, and distraught.

I, as many of us probably do, know people who grow up seeing God as distant or heavy-handed because their fathers were like that when they were growing up. Some blamed their fathers and others blamed both God and their fathers for their pain and misery. When this sort of mindset happens, children are much less likely to turn to God in times of trouble. Instead, they run to someone or something else to deal with the pain and disappointment that may grow inside. We must remember that our irresponsible behavior can have far-reaching and long-lasting consequences and we need to check ourselves very thoroughly. We will take a look at some of the traits that can constitute the makings of an irresponsible father as we go through this section and hopefully you can begin to pinpoint areas that you may need improvement. No father is perfect and we can all stand to improve in one or more areas so do not feel judged, condescended to, or condemned as you read. Simply take note and work towards improving.

The first kind of irresponsible father we will discuss is the kind of man who behaves with wonton recklessness and does things like having children arbitrarily. It may sound a little cliché considering the various daytime and primetime television shows that we have but, in this world, it is not uncommon for men and women to have multiple sexual partners and multiple children with multiple partners. To this point, some people may say, "What is the big deal" or "So what?" and while there are individual or cultural cases like blended families or remarriage, this book particularly focuses on men who father multiple children through irresponsible living.

Inevitably, and somewhat unsurprisingly, there are men who have children they may be unaware of due to the careless one-night stands, illicit affairs, and ongoing fornications. Like all sinful activities, it may seem like fun and games at the moment, however the repercussions fall on everyone. Unfortunately, living outside the will of God means, the children will often suffer most. This can result in children who grow up looking for father figures in all the wrong places, while sabotaging their value, and wondering why they weren't worth the responsibility. This, in turn, opens the door for resentment and bitterness to fester in their hearts. Now, it is important to understand that this isn't the case for everybody as there are many who go on to live wholesome lives. But wouldn't it be better to provide children with a life where they know their fathers and their fathers know them?

GOD WANTS US TO KNOW HIM AND BE KNOWN BY HIM BECAUSE HE LOVES US.

God, as Father, wants us to know Him and to be known by Him because He loves us so much that He knows each and every one of us by name. The Bible says that God knows us so closely that He knows the numbers of hairs we have on your head, so do not be afraid; you are worth more than many sparrows (Luke 12:7). God bears such care for us that He knows the smallest details about us. He knows us and He loves us despite our flaws and shortcomings. You are worth everything to Him and He wants you to see your children in the same way. He gave everything for you and, likewise, every father should be willing to do the same for each of his children. This cannot happen if we do not make the attempt to live in a controlled and disciplined way, being deliberate in making sure that we raise our children in a loving and nurturing environment where we are present and responsible. Even when our children are grown, they will still look to us to be an example of what a responsible father is so we must remain diligent and take care of things as a responsible father should.

    Being a man does not depend on how many women you can get into bed and being a father is more than the number of children you procreate. Being a father comes down to being responsible for the children you have and doing what is best for them and their overall wellbeing. Each family structure is different so, while there is not one way to do this, every father must determine what he will need to do in order to be responsible and set a long-lasting legacy for the children he has. It could be time, finances, being present, or something as simple as a listening ear. Whatever it is, we can see that God demonstrates responsibility towards us and He expects us to do the same. It is time to shed the life of irresponsibility and take care of those who we have been entrusted with to the best of our capability.

Part Two: The Collapse of Fatherhood

THE UNACCOUNTABLE FATHER

—

Another kind of father that exists usually has a relationship of some sort with most, if not all his children however this type of father has a different but equally egregious flaw. This father lacks in taking accountability for his children. This type of father does not provide for his children in one or several means necessary to properly raise a child. This is one of the most glaring and most commonly discussed letdowns of being a father who is failing in his responsibility. On this point, some may think that this pertains primarily to financial accountability and, while that is a large portion, it is not the whole matter. Financial accountability is the most obvious aspect when it comes to provision for our children but there is much more that we may still need to address. Failure regarding accountability can fall into the aspects of finances, being present, emotionally and mentally available, and an active leader of the family; all topics that will be discussed later on.

It is understandable that there are cases where men and fathers are unable to provide due to circumstances out of their control such as hospitalization or incarceration, however there are those who simply choose to neglect providing for their children, citing more important concerns and often conceding support for the well-being of their children to spouses, ex-spouses, grandparents, and the state. In doing this, the father silently communicates to his children that they are not worthy of time, love, or support. To reiterate the Apostle Paul, "But if anyone does not provide for his own family, especially for his own household, he has denied the faith and is worse than an unbeliever" (1 Timothy 5:8). In short, the lowest of lows is when a man chooses to allow his family to suffer so that he can live it up. Accountability will sometimes require us to be humble, vulnerable, and it will require selfless sacrifice for the betterment of our children.

Aside from financial support, a lack of accountability tends to bleed into other avenues, each having a devastating effect on our children and the way they will grow in the future. One avenue comes as a matter of selfishness and a need to satiate a desire rather than instill proper values. This involves taking children to places that they do not need to be, such as bars, rated 'R' movies, and other adult-themed activities. In every situation in which we find ourselves, good judgement needs to be used and exhibited at all times so that our children can see wisdom and follow accordingly—especially within the home. Ensuring that a child's innocence is protected is something that is oftentimes not considered (especially when we really want to do something). As a result, children are then at a greater risk of being exposed to things they may not be ready to see and cannot fully comprehend. In turn, they begin to showcase improprieties, and behavioral patterns they were never meant to hear or see. When this happens, the tendency for a detrimental cycle in a child's life is within arm's reach. Situations not age-appropriate can skew the moral compass of children.

When we are emotionally and mentally accountable to our children, we allow ourselves to be open and available to them. When that happens, our children will be more willing to learn from us because they feel connected to us. Through this connection, we can share our life lessons and wisdom. We can share some of our shortcomings and the lessons we learned from the mistakes we may have made through our lives. Believe it or not, our children will listen and retain that information. They will also be aware of times when we choose to put up walls and shut ourselves off to them. Being accountable to our children teaches them that you are not perfect but you are aware of your struggles and acknowledge that you may make mistakes when raising them but you are trying to get it right. Accountability often leads to open doors in which a father and his children can connect with one another. It shows that you care about their upbringing and what happens to them as they grow into adulthood. It also shows them that you are a vanguard to whom they can come to during the bumpy times in their own lives. In short, there is absolutely no substitute for accountability.

I would like to clarify my point using this example, raising a child is like pouring wet cement that over time begins to harden and as it hardens it is less and less pliable. When the cement is poured improperly, while it is wet, it can easily be corrected but when dried the cement is practically impossible to alter without breaking it. If we pour the cement properly, in teaching our children good and godly values, they will stand to inherit the promises of God. However, if we pour the cement improperly and neglect to correct it, they will stand to face the judgements that God has pronounced just as Eli's sons experienced. As stated before, I truly believe that God is merciful but I do not doubt that He will hold fathers accountable for their parenting or lack thereof.

We, fathers, are accountable for pouring that cement properly and making sure that we do all we can to make sure that it dries well.

Being an accountable father is always the best course when we make mistakes, we can correct them and then show our children a better way to live all the while giving them hope to be able to overcome adversity. As we provide what they need we never want to give them a reason to blame life's difficulties on us and our unwillingness to show accountability because of our selfishness.

I will be the first to admit that it is very hard, especially in this day and age, to raise a child. With so many temptations, distractions, and expectations it can be very overwhelming for many children. It has to be stated that a child who is without a responsible father can struggle to find stability and direction. There might be some who get offended by this statement but God has instituted a mother and a father as the bedrock of the family for a reason. This does not discount children from single parent homes. I stand and applaud the men and women who raise their children by themselves but when a home has a mother and a father it often makes for a much stronger foundation. It is for this reason that Jesus is oftentimes referred to as, "The Rock." He stands strong when we need someone to lean on. Jesus is unyielding in kindness and stability but yet He is firm and uncompromising in showing us how we should live so that we can live long and wholesome lives. This is what He calls for fathers to be to their children and this is what we must be if we are to raise children who are wholesome and strong. This will not happen if we make excuses for being unaccountable fathers. It is time to be accountable, responsible, and honest with ourselves on who we are. We need to put the family first and be the men that we are called to be.

Part Two: The Collapse of Fatherhood

THE ABSENTEE FATHER

—

It is no secret that parenthood can be a delicate road and raising children is no picnic, because no two children are alike and there is no manual on how to raise them. In this day and age with the increasing dependency on technology in addition to church, school, sports, doctor appointments, and the hassle of everyday life, it is necessary that we are attentive and present in our children's lives. There are some fathers who fail in this area in part or as a whole and the number of single parent households worldwide rises as more and more children are finding themselves fatherless.

It is important to note however that not all absenteeism is physical although not physically being there is a much more blatant version of being an inaccessible and unavailable father. Alas, there are some who choose to not only be irresponsible as far as having children and taking care of them but some of them are simply nowhere to be found. Some of these kinds of fathers get to a place where they choose to abandon their families, physically or emotionally, leaving the raising of the children to the charge of someone else. In the minds of some, there are a few solid reasons for a man to leave his family but be assured that none of them are good. God has instituted fathers to be the head of the household and there is no reason that would be approved by this same God for any man to vacate that post.

There are cases of fathers saying things like, "They are better off without me," "I can't take it anymore," "I am tired of this," or "I want to have a life too." As a result, many justify their reasoning for discarding their duties towards their families and, ultimately, the Lord. Now I am not saying that becoming a father or running a household takes away your desires and interests as an individual but our children must always factor into our decision-making. When we do this, we can continually shape the legacy we will be proud of. It will be a legacy that will be passed down through the generations and it can be something which is blessed either by God or cursed by the devil. A man who chooses to walk in the ways of the Lord sets an example of the goodness that comes from serving God but a man who chooses self over service teaches future generations about selfish living.

In order to be fair however, not all absence is necessarily voluntary as some fathers are separated from their children due to work or military duty. We are all human and tomorrow is not guaranteed to anyone. Others tend to make mistakes which can have long lasting legal ramifications in terms of anything ranging from separation to restraining orders to incarceration (if we want to be real because we know these things happen in life). Note however that such circumstances do not completely absolve any father from fatherhood as they can still make the attempt to be a father to their children even from a distance. Incarcerated fathers, for example, can still teach their children the right way to go so that they can learn from their fathers' mistakes and glean wisdom in other areas of life. The decision in large part, when it comes to matters like this, remains with the child if they should look to learn and grow. Regardless, a father needs to do everything within his power to be as present as possible and don't just be present, be involved. Remember that we can be present and visible but absent at the same time and this can hurt just as much.

I will give you an example of this point. There was a successful man I knew who provided for his children and did a wonderful job when it came to financial matters, however when it came to everything else, he was a distant parent. He knew little about their interests and their daily lives. Whenever people asked him about his children, his response was a nonchalant "I don't know, you should ask them." He never attended any of their extracurricular activities and only seemed to care about their grades. You may wonder, where is this father being absent? He provides for his children and they want for nothing. In that respect you are correct in stating that he is fulfilling his financial responsibility and being financially accountable but he is absent in being a part of their daily lives. The message this scenario sends out is that money doesn't fix everything. Good fatherhood requires being a complete part of our children's lives. This means that their interests, their ups and downs, and realizing that absolutely nothing substitutes doing life together with our children. Our love and involvement cannot be limited to our aligned interests (if you and your children have any). When we do this, it shows that our love is limited and conditional.

One common factor of those who choose to abandon their families is something that affects a majority of human beings worldwide—selfishness. Fathers are called to sacrifice for the betterment of their wives and children but this usually requires putting wants, needs, and desires to the back of the line.

Fatherhood requires us to do one of the hardest things; something that goes against our very nature, the need to be selfless. Much of the failure of fatherhood revolves around the need to preserve one's self at the expense of others and changing that mindset does not come naturally to many of us. This is where we need the power of the Holy Spirit to change us and the way that we love our children more than we love ourselves.

Jesus set this perfect example in John 15:13 when He stated, "Greater love has no one than this: to lay down one's life for one's friends" (NIV). If we would do this for our friends imagine how much more we should do for our children. God showed us how much he loved us in the infamous John 3:16, "For God so loved the world that He gave His one and only Son, that whoever believes in Him shall not perish but have eternal life" (NIV). And Jesus fulfilled this scripture when He gave His life for us on Calvary. Jesus the Son and God the Father both exhibited unselfishness. God the Father gave His only begotten Son, the very best and dearest that He has, to heal the sin of the world. He did this despite the pain it would cause to watch His son be rejected, suffer, and die for our sin, both Son and Father were selfless.

GREATER LOVE HAS NO ONE THAN THIS: TO LAY DOWN ONE'S LIFE FOR ONE'S FRIENDS.

In the New Testament, the Apostle Paul speaks further on this issue in 1 Corinthians 13:5 where he states, "Love is not rude, is not selfish, and does not get upset with others. Love does not count up wrongs that have been done" (NCV). Love, selflessness, and forgiveness all go hand in hand and without one of those, we cannot live selfless, fully, and abundant lives in fatherhood. Being present will require all three aspects, but in doing so we demonstrate godliness and exhibit a legacy that honors God and lifts our families up.

It is very important to note that selfish fatherhood does not always run parallel with being absent but it is equally as destructive. An example of such selfishness can be choosing to go golfing rather than attend a child's basketball game, chorus recital, or graduation; it means choosing to pour financial resources into selfish endeavors rather than to spend it on bettering the living of his family. The Bible clearly states that such a person is worse than an unbeliever because it is difficult to lead a family in godliness when such a man continues to walk selfishly. This level of selfishness oftentimes leaves a cycle of betrayal, resentment, pain, and destruction amongst the other members of the family.

Another avenue for fatherly absence comes in the form of ambition. Ambition can be defined as the strong desire to accomplish something or to achieve success at something. This usually requires time, money, and effort. These are all things that play a large part, in varying degrees, into being a good father. As parents it is more than important to look at children as valuable. As stated in Psalm 127:3, "Children are a gift from the LORD; they are a reward from him" (NLT). We live in a world where having a child is seen as an inconvenience, a constriction on our grownup lifestyle and a drain on our wallets but the Bible has made it clear that children, in reality, are a blessing that need to be treasured, valued, and invested in. Many times, however, fathers miss the significance of a child's worth and, although a father's ambition is sometimes done with good intention, the value of a father's children can still fall through the cracks.

Ambition, like fire, when utilized properly and within reasonable limits, is a useful and worthwhile tool however when it is misused can be dangerous and can cause irreparable damage.

Men, by nature, tend to need to be the providers in the home and many (not all) feel a sense of ignominy or shame when they fail. As a result, some men choose to spend hours and hours working hoping to make enough money to give their children everything they want but material things are not what is needed. Children may not always admit this fact but a majority of them want and need to have their fathers present at home. It does not go without notice or understanding that a good father looks to dote on his children but there is a balance that needs to be maintained. Fathers who are excessively gone from the home can, in some cases, be almost compared to those who abandon their families with the only difference being the motive for doing so. This does not include those who have to be out for work, deployment, or means that are out of his control. This does include those who feel like they need to do whatever is needed to climb the social, economic, financial, or business ladder for their ambitions. It may ultimately be a means to bring more money to the home but since it comes at the cost of mis prioritizing the family, it is wrong and it opens doors for spiritual attacks and distancing of family members to occur.

These kinds of ambitious fathers are only interested in bettering their own status for the admiration of themselves, at the expense of time with their children. This can even overflow into the church where a man can spend so much time involved in ministry and other church activities that the time that should be spent with his children are dedicated to other things. While his work in the church will bless others, it can be done at the expense of blessing his own family. It is hard for us to be the spiritual covering for our families when we are not there.

Ministry is what every Christian is called to and this, by no means, is meant to attack or criticize fathers who answer the call to ministry. Fatherhood, in itself is a ministry and it ultimately means that godly service to the family comes before anything and anyone else. We are to minister to our families in accordance with the Word. God wants us to be invested in our children's lives as He is in ours. He is interested in our hobbies, daily programs, jobs, and everything in between and he wants us to do the same. His Word will never lead us astray. Hebrews 4:16 states, "Let us then with confidence draw near to the throne of grace, that we may receive mercy and find grace to help in time of need" (ESV). Similarly, children should be able to have respect for their father and never feel like he is too big, intimidating, or distant for them to have a close relationship with. Fathers must realize that a majority of this is their responsibility to fulfill. Be available to your children as God is to you.

A FATHER SHOULD NEVER BE TOO BIG, INTIMIDATING, OR DISTANT FOR HIS CHILDREN TO HAVE A RELATIONSHIP WITH HIM.

Another avenue by which some fathers have a tendency to be absent is on an emotional level. Men, stereotypically, are not known to be emotional when dealing with issues. While this is not completely true, there is an element that some men can feel the need to demonstrate machismo and thus do not tend to look to attend to emotional issues.

Others may be willing but have never learned to deal with emotional matters and are ill-equipped. As a result, they tend to shy away from it or mishandle it when it arises. This can often result in forgetting that we are representatives of God to the children. This results in children who grow up sometimes directionless and oftentimes embittered wondering if God exists and if He even cares about them.

One form of emotional absence comes in the form of a lack of sympathy or empathy to the things that our children may experience. The reasons for this can be many but a few of them can involve family dynamics, the need to "toughen" our kids up, a lack of patience, and the belief that the child might be exaggerating or embellishing. Additionally, a father might find it difficult to show emotion out of his own upbringing, anger issues, ego, or insecurity that if he should do so his own masculinity might be called into question. His remedy to this? Build walls of security around his emotions.

Fathers fail their children when they do not extend their arms, open their ears, or share their hearts but instead tell them in no uncertain words to "walk it off" and deal with it. As a result, some children grow up to see their fathers as a locked door instead of a haven of safety. The boys grow up thinking that being emotionless is manly. All the while, putting our young girls at risk. Daughters who then grow up to be women, looking in other men for the things she did not get from her father. Why would we want to do that to them?

Sympathetic and emotional absences can also lead to an outward expression of hard-heartedness and an overall callousness that can be active or passive in nature. This can manifest in several ways to include distance (emotional and physical) from family members, refusal to make any changes in lifestyle and behavior to be warmer to family members, and an aggressive tone or body language when attempting to avoid addressing issues. It is imperative and crucial for each father to understand that the one person on earth who is to be warm, open, and caring in the lives of his children is him. In the same way that we want God to treat us, we should do likewise for the children God has entrusted to us.

In a world that sometimes blows with the coldness of arctic winds, no parent should show callousness to his children. When children see that their fathers are hard-hearted and cold, the misconception is that God does not care when we go through hard times or that God does not want to hear about our issues. That cannot be any further from the truth. Even though God knows everything about us, He wants us to tell him everything we are feeling in both good and bad times. He wants to hear from us and he genuinely cares to know how we are doing. In the books of Psalms and Lamentation, the authors spare no feeling in telling God just how they felt. When things were good, they gave God praise, when things weren't so great, they gave praise anyway however they were honest with God about their anguish and their pain. These books became part of the Bible and they show that God is not afraid or offended by our expressions and in similar fashion, we should not be afraid or offended to listen to our children when they come to share an exciting or difficult time in their lives.

I have had the privilege to teach youth and young adults in the church I attend, and what I have learned is that investing in emotional support is crucial for their development. A few students would share that when they would go and talk to their fathers in hopes of some advice or encouragement, they would receive neither on many occasions.

What they had to say was regularly ignored, rejected, and, in some cases, attacked. The emotional indifference left them feeling distant and angry and they became more hesitant in sharing their struggles, ideas, and concerns to their fathers. Some students admitted that they felt misunderstood, and devastated, that their fathers displayed busyness, impatience, or simple lack of desire to understand. Eventually, some of them began to look for role models among the youth leaders while it seemed that they drifted further and further from their fathers. All I could think of during those times is how much these fathers are missing and how much of an influence they could be if they just took the time to listen. Thankfully, God is not that way. Fortunately, we can take note of our failures and make the necessary changes.

SPIRITUAL ABSENCE IS ALSO A WAY BY WHICH SOME FATHERS FAIL THEIR CHILDREN. MORE THAN HALF OF HOUSEHOLDS ARE LED SPIRITUALLY BY THE WOMEN IN THE HOME.

The final form of absenteeism we will discuss describes the fathers who are missing spiritually. God has not called fathers to just be providers and protectors. As I have mentioned already, all fathers are called to be the primary spiritual authority figures in the home and even when the children move out of the house, it is still the responsibility of the father to serve as a spiritual covering over each and every one of his children no matter how far from the Lord they may have run. There are many of us who, known or unknown to us, have been rescued from various situations because of the prayers of godly parents. Prayer is the most powerful tool in our arsenal as Christians because prayer moves the hand of God when it is done in faith and genuine intent. Even those who are not Christians have been known to pray to God in dire times. This shows the power and importance of prayer and as fathers, it is of unmeasurable importance to keep in constant contact with the heavenly father not just in regards to our wants, needs, and desires, but also for direction and blessing over our children and grandchildren as well.

Throughout the Bible and life, it is clear to see that blessings and curses can span generations. In Psalm 100:5, God shows just how holy, righteous, and good He is. King David wrote about the Lord's integrity, "For the LORD is good; his steadfast love endures forever, and his faithfulness to all generations" (ESV). God's holiness is an amazing quality but it should not be taken for granted. In His holiness, God does not refrain from serving justice and allowing us to endure the consequences of our decisions. This is demonstrated in Exodus 34: 6-7 in which God spoke to the Israelites stating, "The LORD passed before him and proclaimed, "The LORD, the LORD, a God merciful and gracious, slow to anger, and abounding in steadfast love and faithfulness, keeping steadfast love for a thousand generations, forgiving iniquity and transgression and sin, but who will by no means clear the guilty, visiting the iniquity of the fathers on the children and the children's children, to the third and the fourth generation" (ESV).

This verse is clear in demonstrating that God is kind and loving and it shows that God wants to bless us even more than we could imagine but He also warns us of what can happen if we choose to go in the opposite direction. All fathers must walk with confidence and purpose but every step must be taken with attentiveness for the sake of his children and the blessings that come from the Lord when the path of godliness is followed. In order for God's promises to be fulfilled we need to actually be present and available. We cannot allow the busyness of life to take us away from God's assurances, we must make time to be with God and allow Him to work through us as a conduit to blessing our children.

Despite God's promise and His warning, the fact is true that many fathers are absent spiritually. In today's world, most children who go to church are taken by their mothers not their fathers. Statistics show that the number of mothers who lead the children to attend church is at about sixty percent. Additionally, if a father does not go to church, even if his wife does, only one child in fifty will become a regular worshipper. That comes out to two percent of children when fathers are not present and do not actively serve as a participant of his children's spiritual upbringing.

If a father does go regularly, between two-thirds and three-quarters of their children will attend church as adults. If a father attends church irregularly, between half and two-thirds of their kids will attend church with some regularity as adults. If a mother does not go to church, but a father does, a minimum of two-thirds of their children will end up attending church. In contrast, if a father does not go to church, but the mother does, on average two-thirds of their children will not ever attend church. In another survey that was done, statistics showed that If the mother is the first to become a Christian, there is a seventeen percent probability everyone else in the household will follow. However, when the father is first, there is over a ninety percent probability everyone else in the household will follow.

I remember several years ago while teaching Sunday school to a group of middle school age boys, I noticed that there were some boys who showed little interest. As time went on, I was able to meet some of the parents who would come and introduce themselves and I began to notice a pattern forming as I met them. I noticed that some of the ones who showed little interest in the class had a tendency to come to church with their mothers and siblings. I remember one particular time when a mother of one of those students came to me and asked me if I could teach her sons to pray. This request left me a bit baffled, as this young man and his brother had been coming to our church for several years and still never learned to pray As I spoke with their mother, I also realized that I had never met the father of these young men and while I do not look to criticize his absence, I see the effect his absence from church had on his sons and their spiritual development. I do not bash parents who are struggling to raise their children but it is important to note that the primary teacher of all godly matters lie in the hands of the parents. While Sunday school teachers are of vital importance and serve as support staff, they should not be the main source for our children's spiritual upbringing. Joshua 24:15 ends with a popular Christian saying "As for me and my house, we will serve the Lord". This was a declaration of a determination made by a father to stand for himself and for his family to serve God. Being the spiritual head of the household is not something new but it is something that God expects of every man who is a father. Let us step up to the plate and determine that we and our families will serve the Lord.

One major reason for the deficit of participation by many fathers however is a partial or total lack of belief or interest in what is being taught in churches. There are many fathers who, as children, may have been forced to go to church and as they got older and more independent, they began to discard that which was taught to them in their younger years in one way or another, or possibly in total. It is also possible that in this busy world we, as a society, are bombarded with information from every direction. A man may begin to experience doubts and slowly slip away from the church as he spends less and less time with the Lord as other things take priority in his life.

To illustrate this point, I know of several men whose children play various sports on travel or club teams. The fact that they play on those teams is not a big deal however the main issue is that they play many of their games on Sunday mornings. As a result, many parents end up missing church in order to attend the games and, realistically for some, Sunday is the only day that they spend with the Lord. Without Sunday services they are at risk of spiritual stagnation and vulnerability to defeat when attacks from the devil come. We are all going to be attacked by the devil, the question is will you be victorious through Jesus Christ or will we fall because we are living in the flesh and trying to do things ourselves? We all go through times of weariness and turmoil but there is no victory in walking away from God. We must prioritize what's important and make sure that our children know that God comes first in everything. Other men may experience a decline in faith over the years or due to a life-changing event such as the death of a loved one, a diagnosis of cancer, or something that may cause him to question God's goodness, control, or even His existence. In times like these, it isn't uncommon for an individual to become angry and this is where the devil moves in with the objective to get the person to blame God.

There is a myriad of reasons why some fathers do not make their spiritual lives a priority. It is important to note that if the father is not excited about God and serving the Lord, his children most likely will not be either and thus he would have failed his mission.

There are other ways in which a father can be absent spiritually. One is to struggle with a lethargic and weary walk with the Lord. Walking with the Lord can sometimes feel like walking up a steep incline or climbing a mountain. It can feel like swimming against the tide or walking into a high-velocity wind. Even when we walk with the Holy Spirit, we can sometimes experience fatigue and, especially if our walk is not airtight, exhaustion. The fact that we can get tired is not the issue, but what we decide to do when we are in such a position does matter for both the father and the family. We can choose to press on in our weariness and trust that the Lord will carry us through the storm and renew our strength as He promised in Isaiah 40:31 where he proclaimed, "but those who hope in the LORD will renew their strength. They will soar on wings like eagles; they will run and not grow weary, they will walk and not be faint" (NIV). Or we can choose to stop, withdraw, or give up altogether. It is much better that we press on so that we do not give up on God's promises and faithfulness or our families and our call to lead them. Our children are always watching and they will follow us in the choices that we make. Do we give up or do we press on? In all things we need to keep in mind that our children are always watching us. Do we reflect Jesus in the way we handle things? Would we be proud to see our children emulate us? I hope so.

When we trust that God will keep to His promise because He is God and He does not lie, we become encouraged that He will not allow us to fall victim to whatever situation we may be facing. As fathers it is important to remember that Satan's war on the family is nonstop and if he can take the father out of the picture, he has accomplished a big objective in taking the family apart.

Please understand that this is an easier task when we are weary and lethargic. Among Christians, there are those who are lulled into such a state and never seem to notice that their prayer lives, devotionals, and other Christ-related activities are no longer as enjoyable, genuine, or even appealing. It is at these times that we need the Holy Spirit to nudge our spirits to awaken us to getting back to a strong relationship with Christ if we are open to it.

When the Holy Spirit alerts a man to his dull walk with the Lord, it is at that point that he will have to make the decision if he wants to be receptive to the Holy Spirit's nudging. If we are honest with ourselves, we sometimes enjoy our spiritual sleepiness and prefer to remain at status quo than to shake ourselves awake and get back to the battle at hand. It is at this time especially that we must look to get back to being godly fathers and spouses in a time when it is increasingly harder to follow the Lord. This is not to criticize, condemn, or discourage fathers who may be struggling in this or other areas but it is to serve as a wakeup call to those who have unconsciously slipped. The battle is real and it is here, whether you want to believe it or not. Going to church is a good thing however, in order to be effective, fathers need to stand in the strength of the Lord and rest in the security and the strength of His power and His promises. This means actually knowing the Lord through a real relationship with Him and not just knowing of him through a weekly church service.

For those who have reservations or those who do not believe, here is a question to mull over in your mind. What do you have to lose by trusting in Jesus Christ and believing that He will work things out for you to become a better father to your children? As the infamous verse John 3:16-17 states, "For God so loved the world that He gave His one and only Son, that everyone who believes in Him shall not perish but have eternal life. For God did not send His Son into the world to condemn the world, but to save the world through Him" (BSB). God loves us so much more than any earthly father could and as a show of that love, He gave us His Son, Jesus Christ, to come, show us God's love, teach us how to imitate God's love, He demonstrated the greatest aspect of love by ultimately dying in our place for our sins and resurrecting as an open show of His victory over sin, Satan, and the grave.

We aren't perfect like the Father but we can be sure that we live and show the same kind of love Jesus showed to people while He was here on Earth. Jesus said "Let the little children come to me, and do not hinder them, for the kingdom of heaven belongs to such as these" (Matthew 19:14). This verse shows in plain text how Jesus (and God the Father) feels about children and if we claim to know and follow Him, as fathers, there is absolutely no reason to not do the same.

IF OUR CHILDREN SEE THAT GOD IS NOT OUR FIRST OPTION, THEY WILL LOOK FOR SOMETHING ELSE TO FILL THE VOID THAT ONLY GOD CAN FILL.

Children, as many people are aware of, are very observant and they see a lot more than they are often given credit for and though they may not say much, their minds are constantly processing. If the message that they see is that God is replaceable, they will come to look to other means for fulfillment and they will deal with issues in manners that are similar to the ways their fathers may have done.

As a result, they will likely fall into the same pit or worse and that is one way that generational cycles of self-destructive behavior begin. It is time, as fathers, to stop being absent from the children and all fathers need to look to put an end to these cycles and get our children on the path for which God created them.

Part Two: The Collapse of Fatherhood

THE DISHONORABLE FATHER

—

To dishonor someone or something is to bring same or disgrace to that person or thing. While God looks at all sin the same, this kind of selfishness is a lot more personal and painful as it involves the joining of two people on multiple levels. In Mark 10: 7-9, Jesus taught about the importance and the sanctity of marriage when He spoke of the union of a man and his wife, "For this reason a man will leave his father and mother and be united to his wife, and the two will become one flesh.' So they are no longer two, but one flesh. Therefore what God has joined together, let man not separate" (BSB). Paul followed up on this teaching by speaking on what it means to have an affair or to live a carnal and reckless life in 1 Corinthians 6:16 "Do you not know that he who unites himself with a prostitute is one with her in body? For it is said, "The two will become one flesh."

You may ask how this relates to fatherhood. An affair is an event involving two consenting adults and it has nothing to do with the kids.

In our everyday world where perversion and the degradation of commitment in marriage is more common and more accepted, we seem to think that we can do whatever we want without consequence. I want you to know that this is a lie that the devil has told to make it seem like it is all just fun, games, and adventure. Let me assure you that there is a day of reckoning where everything we do we will give an account for. When people have affairs or maintain any form of sexual relationship outside of the bonds of marriage, they betray the members of their families who look up to them and furthermore, they spit in the face of God who has ordained the father to be the head of the home and honor the marriage bed with the woman that they promised to be faithful to. Dishonor usually ties into selfishness where we do not think of the lasting damage that is done to a family as a result of our actions. Whether the dishonor is physical (ex. Adultery), emotional (ex. Flirting with another person), or anything else, the message is that what we have either isn't enough or it isn't good enough for us. Either way you sacrifice your family in one way or another. Even for those who may not be believers in Christ, it is still possible to be a dishonorable father by the way that you live.

You may wonder, "How can I tell?" Let me put down a few questions for you to think about. Do you hide things from them? Do you lie to cover up things that you may be doing? Would you be ashamed or uncomfortable if they found out? Does your conscience prick about your choices and decisions? Maybe God is trying to get your attention. This goes beyond just you, it involves your family and can make them victims in your game of selfish and dishonorable living and God is trying to warn you of consequences you and they may face if you don't stop. God is reaching out to you- don't ignore Him.

When a person turns their back on God's ordinance in any way, they inevitably embrace the tactics and dispositions of the devil who says that affairs and fornication are no big deal, everybody does it. When buying into this lie, refusing God's direction, and choosing to do our own thing, the devil then has free reign to systematically dismantle and ultimately destroy the family. The devil will not stop at dealing with just you if given the chance because his purpose is destruction and as mentioned previously, he hates the family with a passion and will do anything to destroy it if he can. We need to avoid godless living and focus on our children who need to be kept in prayer daily because they are the future and they are the next legacy of previous generations.

This cannot happen if the legacy left demonstrates that living a carnal irresponsible life yields the blessings of God. It is a lie and God does not give his blessings to us when we live dishonorably. When we live honorably, especially if we are Christians, we bring honor to God and to His name and one thing that God values highly is His name. Reputations are often tied to a person's name whether it is for good reasons or for bad ones and one thing that God wants us to be is honoring to our families and those around us. This means marital faithfulness and integrity to every situation that we encounter whether we have something to gain from it or not. Remember, eyes are always watching what we do, always. Honor lifts up the family and the legacy left behind, while dishonor causes a family name to drag through the mud. Do you care which one applies to yours? I pray you choose to live honorably and lift the family and the name of the Lord through your life decisions.

Part Two: The Collapse of Fatherhood

THE DOMINEERING FATHER

—

A domineering person by definition is someone who asserts their will over others with an attitude of arrogance. The domineering father has a tendency to be somewhat heavy-handed (although not always physically) which can provide a tense and very pressure-filled environment. Typically, when most people think of the stereotypical domineering father, they think of a man who tends to be an alcoholic or someone who is visibly intimidating but, while this happens, is not the only way to be domineering. Being a domineering father oftentimes has to do with the attitude that is portrayed. A domineering father could wear a suit as much as he could wear slacks or jeans. He could work in an office as much as he could work in a bar or an auto shop. A domineering father can come from any walk of life and can live in any kind of household. The basis is all in the approach and mannerism in which the father runs things and operates within his family and the ultimate effect it has on the members of the home.

Although there are many characteristics to a domineering father, in this book, we will focus on a few of the main ones starting with the father whose mindset towards his family is that he alone is in control. Throughout this book it has been addressed over and over that the father is the head of the home and he is responsible for what happens to his family within his influence. Nonetheless, when a man's thought pattern overflows into the arena of authoritarian control it becomes a dangerous place. Fathers who run their families through such control do not show love to their children and they do not set an example for future generations. A controlling father does not allow his children to grow or develop in the nurturing home but instead he demands that a child should grow in a certain way regardless of the child's strengths, weaknesses, interests, or struggles.

In order to make a better visual of this point I would like to provide an illustration. Think of raising your children as holding them in an open hand versus a closed fist. In both scenarios the child does not fall but one allows the supportive growth of the child in a nurturing and open environment under the watchful eye of a loving father. The other allows little to no freedom to move, expand, or grow beyond what is allowed by the fist with limited opportunity for personal development. As fathers we may have good intentions and may truly mean well but we are always to remember that we all have been given gifts and talents by the Lord and not all our gifts are the same.

We all have different strengths and weaknesses; where one person might be an introvert, another might be an extrovert or where one person may be a good artist or a good dancer or leader, another might be a good teacher, doctor, or IT technician. None of these are wrong but these talents need to be nurtured and with a controlling father such nurture is unlikely, especially in the cases where the father does not believe a certain talent to be useful or beneficial. When a father is domineering, criticism is a regular occurrence and harsh words can crush a child's dream and ability to fulfill the plan that God may have had for the child. Fathers, we need to be careful not to crush our children's dreams. Open your hands, nurture your children, and their visions, and let them grow as God has planned for their lives. Let us guide and inspire not intimidate. You never know what God's plans are for your child but your legacy will be tied to it one way or another.

WE NEED TO REMEMBER THAT GOD HAS GIVEN ALL DIFFERENT GIFTS. OUR CHILDREN'S GIFTS MIGHT NOT BE WHAT WE WOULD PREFER BUT ALL GIFTS ARE FOR GOD'S GLORY. IT IS OUR JOB TO NURTURE THOSE GIFTS NOT TO CRUSH THEM.

A domineering father can create an atmosphere of fear and anger for his children because such a man often brings with him an air of restriction in which there are usually consequences for any deviation from the expectation he has set before them. Some may do this as a means to live vicariously through their children and, by doing this, a father robs his children of the opportunity to explore life for themselves and to develop their own persona. Such men instead insist that the development of his children operate according to his plan for their lives. An example of this would be a father who tells his children what profession they will have or what university they will attend and what they will study or dictating what interests he wants them to have.

These are simply examples and I am sure that you may come up with a few more but hopefully you get the big picture. Please understand that a good father is very much involved in every step of his children's lives and it is every father's job to offer guidance and support but dictating a child's every move can only look to lead to a rebellious, resentful, or disastrous end.

Understand that raising a child and controlling a child are two different things with two different results. As previously stated, apart from God, no father is perfect but any good father will provide guidance to his children in an attempt to ensure that they develop properly. Ultimately, the decision belongs to the child whether they will follow or rebel against the wisdom that has been imparted to them. Imparting knowledge is the father's job, accepting or rejecting that knowledge is solely up to the child and God will judge both accordingly.

God Himself provides each and every one of us with gifts and talents with a plan for each one of our lives, however He has also imparted us with the special gift of free will. God gives us the choice to choose if we will adhere to biblical truths and the promises God has offered to those who have chosen to follow him or if we will look to follow our own way. In the book of Proverbs 14:12, God addresses this situation clearly where it is written, "There is a way that appears to be right, but in the end, it leads to death." He also offers His guidance in Deuteronomy 30:19, "This day I call the heavens and the earth as witnesses against you that I have set before you life and death, blessings and curses. Now choose life, so that you and your children may live." He will give us the self-will to choose but the consequences are ours, although God is always there to pick us up when we fail. In the same way we need to be watchful and diligent. We must learn to work in conjunction with the leading of the Holy Spirit, in the growth of our children allowing them room and opportunity to grow into the person who God has created them to be. All the while, serving as a barrier when it is clear that the child is going down a path that leads to death.

Control goes along with the next characteristic of a domineering father. This type of father is adamant about not being questioned as he has a tendency to see questioning as an affront to his authority. In the minds of some men, the questioning of his decision-making can be seen as disrespectful and a sign of a lack of confidence in him or his intelligence to make good decisions. This, in turn, can trigger a perceived attack on his ego and for many men, messing with ego is a very dangerous place to be. In a world where everybody has an opinion, a voice, and the sense or impression that every thought needs to be vocalized, it is easy to question authority. In the right context it is not always wrong but it must be done respectfully and with godly motives. In the mind of a domineering father, many sorts of opposition are unacceptable practices and at the root of it, he may see it as rebellion. It is at this point that every father needs to be careful to understand the reason for the questioning because, while he is appointed as the head of the household and he is accountable to God for his leading of the family, he is not autonomous unto himself. Not all questioning is bad and not all of it is meant to rebel against his intellect or decision-making paradigm. Some questions are for his own good as well as the good of the family. In the same way, a head of state has advisors, I truly believe that it is always good to hear other ideas or questions to make sure that as fathers we use every resource in making the best decisions for the good of the family.

A family is a unit for a reason and in a family dynamic, while the ultimate decision should be on the father's shoulders (although mothers have just as much responsibility), children should not be afraid to speak. When a father carries the mentality of never having his authority questioned, he becomes a relatively unapproachable authority figure and a poor representation of what God is like to us. In Hebrews 4:16, we are encouraged to come BOLDLY before the throne of grace so that we may receive mercy and find grace to help us in our time of need. When we genuinely come to God's throne, He will give us the opportunity to share our wants, needs, desires, even our hurts and grievances without fear of punishment. Likewise, we as fathers should be willing to listen to the hearts of our children whether they are filled with joy or pain and, most importantly, we should not feel like we need to control the situation. As children grow, they must be allowed to flourish and fathers need to nurture but guard this growth not control it.

An example of this point is when God was going to destroy the city of Sodom for its wickedness and Abraham spoke to God about it because of his nephew Lot who happened to reside in the city. Abraham reverently spoke to God who eventually agreed to spare the city if only ten righteous men could be found in the city. Sadly, the ten were not found and God destroyed Sodom after evacuating Lot and his family from the city. It is important to note however that God as the father, did not see Abraham's request as an affront to his sovereignty. Neither was Abraham fearful to approach God with his proposal to spare a condemned city. May every father hope to have such a relationship with his children for the betterment of his children and his own internal well-being. Being domineering, closes so many doors and destroys many more relationships because it places the father out of the reach of his children. God, on the other hand, is very approachable. So we as godly men, should work on being approachable as well.

The domineering father also comes in another fashion that ties in with the controlling and authoritarian approach. This approach states, "it's my way or the highway." Which usually goes hand-in-hand with the father who does not like for his authority to be questioned. An individual who falls into this category usually has a fear of the unknown, a hard time with trying new things, admitting when they are wrong or showing ignorance and preferring stagnant comfort. Domineering fathers tend to be reluctant to listen to any type of advice or opinion that may deviate from their own. Children in such relationships are usually reprimanded and even suffer at the hands of these domineering fathers. When a father employs the "my way or the highway" method of parenting, he teaches his children to be inflexible. Children learn limited ways of managing situations and coping internally when help is out of the question.

Forcing a person to conform to one way of doing things never allows the individual or the relationship between a father and a child to grow. This mindset often has a tendency to sow seeds of resentment as it gives children the sense that they are unable to suggest anything innovative. In the Bible, it says that we are to train up a child in the way that they should go; this does not mean that we are to force them into a particular way of thinking. The verse simply means that we are to guide and instruct them in direction that they should be growing, while being willing to foster an environment to allow the children the freedom to grow according to the truths God has given through the Bible.

As fathers, it is our duty to train our children up in the ways of God and the Word of God so that when they get older, they will not turn their back on Him. We understand the good and the benefit of serving the Lord and we want the best for our children, so we teach them to trust in God as Lord and Jesus as our Savior.

What we do not do is tell them how they will serve the Lord. When we try to coerce them or impose upon them the way that they should serve, we have missed the objective of that verse. As previously stated, God has given us all different talents and He has called us all to a specific purpose. What God asks is that we use the talents He has given us to glorify Him according to His will.

By raising children in the ways of the Lord, a father teaches his child to hear and follow the instruction of God. In saying this, it is important that the will of God might differ from the desire of the father for his child. A good father will understand this and bow to the will of God over his own will for his child. By doing this, he submits his will and teaches his child to submit his/her will to a far more perfect father than any one of us could be—who undoubtedly has a much better plan for their lives than we could ever imagine. The big question is how will we achieve this goal if we are domineering and inflexible to change from what we are familiar with or used to? Remember that if God is involved, any change is for the better.

As fathers it is important to share our wisdom and teach our children the things that will help them to be successful, contributing members of society. That will never happen if we distance them through hard-heartedness and hard-headedness caused by the "my way or the highway" mentality. God does not employ this approach as He gives us His Word in the Bible. Throughout the pages, God provides advice and commandments, however He has also given us free will. Through free will we have the option to follow or not, but God will not force us to take His Word. Nonetheless, consequences do follow if we choose to do things in our own strength. Some may say that God uses the, "my way or the highway" approach, but he does not. In all of our flaws, God is kind, loving, and always provides helpful feedback for our future choices. Notwithstanding, every choice we make has consequences. It is up to us to decide how we will use our knowledge of who God is.

As the Bible mentions, God is the very source of heaven's existence and without Him, heaven does not exist. When we freely choose to reject Him, we are purposely choosing to not want to be with Him, and since God is a gentleman, He will not force us to do anything we don't want to do. Therefore, free will is at our disposal. When we choose to be outside of His will and separated from His love, we rob ourselves of eternal peace and joy in Heaven. We undoubtedly choose hell. Hell is the absence of God along with His grace, mercy, and forgiveness. Hence, why we can't blame God if we refuse Him and go to hell. He has given us Jesus as our substitute and only He can save us from eternal punishment through our acceptance of Him as Lord and Savior.

When we reject our Savior's payment for our sin, we are left with one option and that is to pay for our own sin, a debt that we will never be able to pay. In His love He guides us but, in His love, He allows us to choose to accept or reject Him. He always gives us a chance to come to Him whenever we ask Him to take our sin and we choose to make Him our Savior. When it comes to the "my way or the highway" approach, God invites you to life and victory but He will allow us to do what we want as long as we know that we will be accountable to Him for the life that we live. Heaven is wherever God is while hell is wherever God's presence, love, and forgiveness is absent. Let Him lead you and love you so that you can enjoy life while you are here and enjoy eternity even more when you get to the other side. Know that God is holy which means one who is worthy of complete devotion as one perfect in goodness and righteousness.

Therefore, He cannot be in the presence of sin which is missing the mark or a transgression of divine law. When we reject God, we choose sin thereby disqualifying ourselves from being with Him. Ultimately, it is not God saying "My way or the highway", it is us telling God that we don't want Him. Think about that.

The final section to be addressed in the matter of a domineering father addresses matters of, "do as I say not as I do." This practice, in short, is hypocrisy. Throughout history people have been subjected to ever-changing rules of do's and don'ts while those enforcing the rules seem to skate through life without a care in the world. In the Bible, Jesus confronted the teachers of the law on several occasions for this reason. There was the incident of the teachers of the law accusing Jesus of working on the God ordained day of rest which is known as the Sabbath (Luke 14), the teaching and the call to not judge one another (Matthew 4-5), and the infamous story of Mary Magdalene, the woman caught in adultery whom Jesus forgave but still had to deal with those who wanted her dead (John 8). In each one of these scenarios, Jesus did not teach one thing and do another, He lived every lesson that he taught and as fathers, Jesus calls each of us to do the same.

Again, children will always look at the actions of their parents more than they will necessarily listen to their words. They look to see if we actually follow what we preach and if it doesn't, oftentimes rebellion is quick to ensue. If parents explain their own struggles to their children, they tend to be more understanding and learn from their parent's mistakes. While others may admire their parent's vulnerability, they may fall into the same temptation or mistake. Unfortunately, parents who struggle with substance abuse for example, may warn their kids of the effects, but their children may fall into it anyway. These kinds of parents acknowledge their shortcomings and try their very best to guide their children. Others continue will continue to live as they want and expect their kids to do as they "say" and not as they "do." This could be perceived as a double standard to the child, hence the rebellion. In this section, I will state that both fathers and mothers are equally culpable.

As an example, there are some parents I know, some of them friends, who tell their children to be mindful of their language and to control their physical aggression but fail to do so themselves. Some find themselves yelling and using hostile tones, others find themselves cursing and using other foul language, and in rare cases, I have seen parents grab things and throw them around or break them altogether. As a result, the children emulate the, "do as I do" mentality and copy the behavior of their parents. Afterall, the old saying goes, "the fruit doesn't fall far from the tree". Even in the Bible, Jesus said that He saw the Father always working so He too was always working. His actions were always focused on what He saw the Father do because He knew His life would glorify the Father if He did what His Father did. Imagine if the Father lived in one way and expected Jesus to live another. It would be utter chaos and the love and the legacy of the Father would have been lost, as would we, because there would be no salvation for us.

By teaching according to "do as I say, not as I do," a father communicates that a child should just do what he/she is told and not follow what they may see their father do. By doing this, a father absolves himself of setting an example for his children while hoping to have them live as he would have them. There are some fathers (and mothers) who look to try to portray a character that absolves them of their true nature through twofaced behavior.

This is just as bad as, "I say not as I do" because it displays a false narrative of who the individual is both as a father and as a man. This fake persona is also something that a child notices and it has had an adverse effect on many relationships between fathers and their children in today's world and for many years' past.

    An example of this could be the father that is belligerent and berates his children on the way to church and as soon as they step into the church building, their demeanor changes. They put on a cheerful or humble facade to the rest of the parishioners they may encounter over the day and once service is over, they go back to being surly, mean-spirited, and strict. Another example could be the father who is abusive, dismissive, or condescending when they are at home but in public they put on a different face and personality. Several of the middle school, high school, and university students I have taught over my years of service in the youth group have shared that this example is an all-too-common cause of rifting between them and their parents. As a result, some of them made the decision to stop attending church altogether because they could not stand the hypocrisy.

    When a child sees their father do this, ultimately, they are seeing a father who lives by a double standard. In the eyes of his child, he lives hypocritically by laying down rules, regulations, and expectations from his children while holding himself to a different set. In essence the children have nothing to aspire to and no paternal model to follow. This will eventually lead to a breakdown in respect and an ultimate degradation of the relationship. Our relationship with our children is something that God takes very seriously. In Matthew 18:6, Jesus is talking to a crowd and He makes the statement, "If anyone causes one of these little ones-those who believe in me- to stumble (or fall into sin), it would be better for them to have a large millstone hung around their neck and to be drowned in the depths of the sea." Jesus, in this verse, mentions little ones who are children and when Jesus mentions anyone, He means anyone but for the sake of this book we will focus on us as fathers. Jesus says that as fathers, if the way we behave, live, or treat them causes them to fall away from following Him (ex. No longer attending church or church-related activities) and live in sin, He will get involved and deal with us accordingly. I know that it seems harsh for God to propose such punishment as hanging a millstone around that person's neck and allowing them to drown in the sea, but it shows clearly that our role as fathers is once again something God takes very seriously and so should we. I cannot stress this enough.

The Bible tells us that we are to follow Christ who came as an example of God the Father. As we read through the life of the Lord Jesus, there is no place that He calls for us to do things that He did not do Himself. He called us to forgive one another and He died on Calvary's cross and rose on the third day so that we could be forgiven. He calls for us to love one another and He died for our sins out of love. He lived (and still lives) a life of love and forgiveness and He calls us to do the same. This is the ultimate example of, "do as I do." As Jesus took this way of living we who want to be good fathers need to ensure that all our words and instructions are backed up by our actions. Only then will our children be able to mimic a healthy example of a man. Remember, it is easier to talk the talk than to walk the walk and children will often follow in the footsteps of their fathers so walk as you talk and raise a good legacy in the next generation.

Part Two: The Collapse of Fatherhood

THE ABUSIVE FATHER

—

The abusive father is the next type of father flaw that exists in the world and the next to be discussed in this book. The definition of abuse is to use wrongly or improperly; misuse; to treat in a harmful, injurious, or offensive way; to speak insultingly, harshly, and unjustly to or about; revile; malign. Each one of the definitions for abuse are all very relevant to the upbringing some children endure, in some cases, over a lifetime. Not all abuse is overt and not all abuse is violent but all abuse inflicts some sort of damage on the individual to whom it is directed and this too leads to rebellion, anger, resentment, bitterness, and despondency in a child. It is important to remember that God is love and part of love is discipline whenever needed as referenced in Proverbs 3:12 and again in Hebrews 12:6-11, where it is mentioned that the Lord disciplines those He loves because He cares and wants to make us like Him in our nature and thinking. If God did not love us, there would be no discipline to correct us, only judgement and punishment for what we have done. His discipline, while unpleasant, is designed to build us up and in no place is it mentioned that God disciplines us maliciously or with evil intent.

God is good. God is holy. God wants to mold us. There are many who take God's discipline and become bitter, not better, and in doing so they miss what God has planned for them.

NOT ALL ABUSE IS OVERT AND NOT ALL ABUSE IS VIOLENT BUT ALL ABUSE IS DAMAGING TO WHOEVER IT IS DIRECTED AT.

The Bible specifically mentions the word "chastisement" in the way that God deals with us in accordance with something sinful we have done or are currently doing. Some may say that the chastisement of God is abuse, however God's chastisement comes with discipline and an objective. There are men who were raised or taught to believe that being a strong father meant to have a strong will and a heavy hand. For some, spanking and other physical forms of punishment or harsh words were not uncommon. For some, physical punishment was usually a first response to address any type of misbehavior and with this experience as boys, some fathers believe in the philosophy of tough love. However, there is one key thing to note between abuse and chastisement: discipline. Abuse is done with the intent of inflicting as much pain as is deemed by the parent for the offense committed by the child. Some use it as a deterrent while some use it to "toughen up" the child while others use it as a means to pacify their anger and frustration. This however can also produce disastrous results if not handled carefully and with affection.

CHASTISEMENT WITHOUT LOVE OR THE PURPOSE OF DISCIPLINE IS PURELY JUST PUNISHMENT.

As a father, all reprimand should be done with discipline in mind and it should be done out of love not anger. Chastisement without love is simply punishment and a father who punishes, not disciplines, his children only looks to sow seeds of wrath and provocation. He does not help his children to grow or draw them close in relationship with himself but instead he pushes them away while creating a space of negativity between them. As a reminder, the characteristics that children see in their earthly fathers they will knowingly or unknowingly attribute to the heavenly father. In this case, if a child sees a father who seems to delight in punishment to appease his own imperfect anger, they might attribute that characteristic to a holy God who deals with our sin and, sometimes, that means pain but it is temporary and it is done to help us deal with our sin. However, God NEVER allows us to stay in our mess unless we choose to. God forgives our sins and even though He does not always remove the consequences of our actions, He is not abusive or distant and He does not leave us to figure it out all alone. As representations for God on earth, we also need to allow our children to grow and learn while providing discipline wherever needed. Please note that there may be times for firm handling of a child or situation they may be involved in but all discipline must be carried out in love and with the attitude of correction not frustration.

As a good father, it is important to know why we are disciplining the child and also for the child to understand why they are being chastised. In this way, the father and child can understand one another and even if the child disagrees, the father is able to take the opportunity to offer guidance for any future occurrences while correcting current behaviors. Chastisement however, must be administered sensibly and judiciously and it must ALWAYS follow a fair assessment and consideration of a situation or circumstance.

Children require patience and understanding and not all fathers are equipped with either characteristic which can eventually lead to frustrations that sometimes end up being taken out on the children. An example could be a father who sees his child stepping out of line and causing trouble or embarrassment to him. Consequently, he takes his frustration or displeasure out on the child. No matter the reason, punishment is not what God intends for any of us to suffer. He does not stand over us waiting for us to make a mistake so that He can deliver His judgement, but He would rather have us endure so that we can be more like Christ. Godly discipline sometimes brings discomfort but no pain goes to waste when God is involved, if we trust in Him.

The saying goes, "Violence begets violence" and for fathers who punish their children needlessly or excessively, the seeds for a cycle of violence are being planted. The Apostle Paul addresses this matter in Colossians 3:21, "Fathers, do not embitter your children, or they will become discouraged." The word embittered means that the relationship between father and child becomes sharp or pungent and the attitude of the child towards the father becomes resentful. None of these things signals the kind of relationship God would want for fathers and their children to have. Abuse is never okay and it will never foster a good relationship or legacy. Why would you want to leave a legacy of abuse behind? It is time to break the cycle and start anew.

Despite stereotypical beliefs about abuse, it is not always physical in nature. As human beings we are created to have emotions and a mental capacity much higher than the animal kingdom, so we can reason and perform our daily functions to the glory of the God who made us in His image. Unfortunately, this is another avenue that some fathers use to address matters with their children. However, the path of emotional and mental abuse is also one that can quickly kill and destroy a relationship. Emotional abuse is defined as, "any act including confinement, isolation, verbal assault, humiliation, intimidation, infantilization, or any other treatment which may diminish the sense of identity, dignity, and self-worth." This type of abuse covers a wide span of indicators that many people might not consider when engaging in them and several of them will be covered in this section of the book.

It is very important to understand that abuse comes in many forms. Some are overt and blatant while some are more subtle but equally as devastating but for this book we will focus on the emotional and mental aspects of abuse and its effect on the family. Emotionally and mentally abusive fathers approach things in subtle or blatantly damaging ways. As stated before, humans are created to be emotional beings and so there are times when we will raise our voices and yell. However, in some cases it is done as a means of intimidation. For some fathers it is done as a means to toughen up their children and while on the outside it might work, on the inside it causes damage of various kinds. As a side note to all fathers, yelling, cursing, and swearing does not make you a man as society would have us believe. The Apostle Paul addressed this in Ephesians 4:29 when he said, "Let no corrupting talk come out of your mouths, but only such as is good for building up, as fits the occasion, that it may give grace to those who hear" (ESV) and again in Colossians 3:8, "But now you must put them all away: anger, wrath, malice, slander, and obscene talk from your mouth." Jesus Himself also spoke on this issue as referenced in Luke 6:45(b) "for out of the abundance of the heart his mouth speaks" (ESV).

Paul spoke on the fact that we should be careful with the words that come out of our mouths and that we should be edifying and uplifting to the people who hear our voice, but the Lord Jesus explained why we should refrain from bad language. He said that the words we speak ultimately reveal who we are on the inside and the state of our hearts. Fathers who feel that in order to run their homes effectively need to yell, swear, threaten, and intimidate their children do not shine the light of Christ that they are supposed to represent. Instead, they reveal their pain, resentment, and overall darkness within. In addition, some children learn that the only way things get done is through aggression and intimidation thereby perpetuating a destructive cycle.

On the opposite side of this type of abuse, instead of yelling, shouting, swearing, and intimidating language there is ignoring, isolation, exclusion, and comparison. Some fathers are not big on raising their voices, others are not so big on being hands-on. Some fathers are simply apathetic and indifferent so they avoid much of the conflict and resort to silence. In the case of some families, fathers tend to favor a certain child or certain children over others in which they may cause resentment among the others towards that child or children and anger towards the father for having isolated, excluded, and compared his children one to another. It isn't uncommon to hear a father who may be frustrated (though not always) say something like, "why can't you be like your brother or sister?" and sometimes fathers even compare their children to other peoples' children.

When we isolate, exclude, or compare our children we marginalize and ruin their psyche. This is why some family members grow to have animosity towards one another. The weeds of bitterness dig deep within the garden of relationship. Fathers, we need to make sure that we don't open the doors to the devil, especially, with our mouths. We must also make sure that we are building our children up and not tearing them down. It is time to break the cycle of abuse and be more like the family God intends for us to have.

WHEN WE EXCLUDE AND COMPARE OUR CHILDREN, WE PORTRAY THE IDEA THAT WE DON'T BELIEVE THAT THEY ARE GOOD ENOUGH.

In some situations, fathers isolate and limit children from friends, social media, and fun activities. In the proper context, such things are a father's responsibility for the sake of the child's upbringing, but when the child is restricted then it becomes a questionable situation. Though this section is not geared to dictate how to be a father, it is in fact to inform the dangers of isolating children. Which can produce feelings of loneliness, inadequacy, poor communication with others, and low self-esteem, among a plethora of other concerns.

For the first year and a half in the university, I was out partying, making up for things I felt like I had missed out on growing up.

I was free from all of the rules back home. I finally had a taste of freedom and I did not want to let it go. While I didn't smoke, try drugs or anything like that, my party life and walk with God were becoming blurred. Thankfully, by God's grace I was able to leave the party scene, have friends, and still be myself. God's conviction upon my life was heavy and loud. Nevertheless, I chose God. The party life was fun but I knew God was better. As I look back to my partying days, I realize that much of what I did was attributed to the feelings of loneliness, inadequacy, and low self-esteem. Now I want to note that I came from a good Christian home with hardworking parents who provided for my siblings and I but I lived much of my life sheltered. I just wanted to breathe and many more of my party friends also wanted the same. Most of them shared they too were sheltered from life and they wanted, like me, to unwind and have fun. I then wondered how much different our lives would have been if we were given a chance to explore and grow a little bit. As caring and loving parents, we must let our children make their own life choices as they get older. Controlling every part of their life isn't healthy for their development and neither is the emotional damage inflicted.

The side effects of sheltering can be lifelong. On the emotional side, the insight is that social support is associated with depression, which if severe and untreated, is associated with increasing disability, loss of weight, disturbed sleep and thoughts of suicide or the actual act of committing suicide. Loneliness can also lead to a self-defeating sense of hopelessness and helplessness that can perpetuate isolation. It can become a vicious, unrelenting cycle.

As a child grows, continued isolation, ignoring of a child or comparison will cause the hurt to ferment and turn into anger and bitterness which will put more and more distance between father and child. When things like this happen, there is usually responsibility on both sides, but we as fathers need to honestly speculate and deliberate how much of the distance in the relationship comes as a result of our actions. Have you excluded or ignored your children? Have you shown preference for one over another? Do you open your arms to one while keeping the others at arm's length? Take a moment to be honest and if you have done something like that, it is time to make some amends and start the healing process.

While this is a big problem with fathers today, this is not a new occurrence however as even men in the Bible were known to have had their favorites. The outcomes have not always been good even though God, in His wisdom, worked things out to the benefit of all. Men like Isaac who favored Esau over Jacob, Jacob who favored Joseph, and even King David chose his son Solomon to be king after his death over the others. All the aforementioned events led to conflict and hostility within the family through Esau plotting to kill his brother, Joseph being sold by his own brothers into slavery, and a civil war within the royal family amongst David's children. God took each situation and made beauty from the ashes, caused by the sins of the fathers. Esau and Jacob eventually reconciled and resolved their issues, God used Joseph through the trials of his slavery and eventual promotion to second in command of Egypt to save the life of millions, and through the line of King David came our Lord Jesus Christ. Note that although God can take any bad situation and turn it into something amazing it does not give any father license to do anything he wants.

In all sections that have been mentioned in regards to areas where fathers tend to falter, there is a dangerous and concerning aspect to failing fathers—denial and deflection. The ultimate goal, when denial or deflection is at work, is for the father to not address or even admit his shortcomings or take any responsibility for his comments or actions. In some cases, the father even goes as far as to blame the victim of his abuse using excuses like, "You got what you deserved" or "You made me do it." He refuses to take responsibility and apologizes for nothing at all. This is simply pride at work which can have devastating effects.

This pitfall has the potential to irreparably damage the relationship between a father and his children. However, it is important to remember that the Bible speaks repeatedly about our duty to one day give an account to a holy God for our actions. In Matthew 12:36, the Lord Jesus confirms this fact when He said, "I tell you, on the Day of Judgment people will give account for every careless word they speak" (ESV). The Apostle Paul reiterates this warning in his second letter to the Corinthians where he states, "For we must all stand before Christ to be judged. We will each receive whatever we deserve for the good or evil we have done in this earthly body" (2 Cor. 5:10, NLT). The Apostle Peter, who was a close disciple of Jesus corroborated with Paul in 1 Peter 4:5 with this verse, "But remember that they will have to face God, who will judge everyone, both the living and the dead" (ESV). This list of verses is simply meant to serve as a notification that God is serious about the way we live. For the sake of this book, the verses will be used to address the behavior of fathers towards their children. Each father will stand before Jesus who sits on the throne of judgement and he will give an account for his treatment of his children. For each mistreatment of his children, each father will have to explain why he did it. Therefore, each father is to walk in fear and trembling of that day and look to the Bible for examples of how to be better fathers.

Abuse is hurtful, it is humiliating, it causes rifts and divides families, and it can start (or continue) a destructive legacy that lasts for generations. When it comes to issues of abuse, fathers need to understand that this is such an important issue. God speaks on it in Ephesians 6:4, "Fathers, do not provoke your children to anger by the way you treat them. Rather, bring them up with the discipline and instruction that comes from the Lord" (NLT). God cares so much that in this one verse He gives an instruction on what not to do and then He gives instruction on what to do and how to do that as well.

ABUSE IS HURTFUL, IT IS HUMILIATING, IT CAUSES RIFTS AND DIVIDES FAMILIES, AND IT CAN START A DESTRUCTIVE CYCLE THAT LASTS FOR GENERATIONS.

Beyond directly abusing our children, fathers can also indirectly cause damage through abusing others close to them. This can include relatives, siblings, and mothers. Abuse of a child's mother can have an equal effect on the child as if it were happening directly to him or her. Whether the mother is your spouse or not, she is the mother of the child and any form of abuse can have a devastating and long-lasting effect on the upbringing of the child. While God prefers that men and women who have children are married and remain so, we live in a fallen world and things don't always go the way that God would want for us. In our sinfulness and God's grace in giving us free will, we make these decisions and those decisions have consequences. When it comes to matters of abuse there is little difference on the sentiment a child may feel and the effect that it will have on a child from their younger years all the way through adulthood.

We are called to love one another and bear one another's burdens and this cannot be done if there is no love or conditional love in you. If you need help and or prayer, there are men groups in church that can encourage you, counsel you, and hold you accountable—you are not alone.

The final topic on this matter intertwines heavily with the previous two. We have the propensity to sin with our bodies, mind, heart, and words. The saying, "Sticks and stones may break my bones but words will never hurt me" , in my opinion is one of the most erroneous statements passed down from generation to generation. Words are powerful and they can build or destroy; they can bless or curse; they can bring life or bring death. The book of James is largely devoted to this issue. Words can have a lasting effect on a person and even for those who do not believe, words can open doors to the spiritual, allowing angels or demons to pour in and either bless or defile a person's life.

GOD DOES NOT CRITICIZE OR DEMEAN US BUT HE WILL DEVOTEDLY CONVICT US WHEN WE GET OUT OF HIS WILL.

As a father there is a vast difference to the effect we can have over our children with our words. A verbally abusive father is a man who uses his words as weapons to hurt his children, whether he realizes it or not. For some fathers this is done in the form of name-calling, insults, condescension, and mockery where fathers in essence, take shots at their children out of frustrations, indifference, or because it was the environment that they themselves were brought up in. None of these reasons are acceptable despite what may be shown on television or what society may dictate. Words can be weapons that can destroy a life if used carelessly. We must always, use our words to build up our children, not tear them down.

We all get angry, but that is not an excuse to verbally abuse anyone, especially our children. Consistently speaking in anger and with hostile words can be particularly damaging to a child. Many times, the child may begin to experience and develop negative emotions of their own. In the book of Proverbs 15:1, King Solomon addresses this very issue where it is written, "A gentle answer makes anger disappear, but a rough answer makes it grow" (ERV). Ultimately, words spoken with harshness, hostility, and anger, provokes a child's anger to grow against his or her parent. This is the very opposite picture of what God has in mind for His vision for the family. Nevertheless, anger and discord within a family delights the devil who as previously stated, wants nothing more than to cause strife and dissension within the home.

Anger is like fire, when unwatched it can cause copious amounts of damage leaving a smoldering wreckage in its wake. Trying to build a relationship in a verbally abusive home is like trying to construct a house in the middle of an inferno—it won't last. So, what is a person to do? Fathers, the answer is simple: uncover your past trauma and identify what is causing you to inflict such pain into your child. Identify it, assess it, and improve. If you are truly driven to improve your relationship with your children, it is absolutely necessary to make sure that prayer (which is always an important and essential first step) becomes more of a priority. We need to get together and be a good influence to one another while walking in godliness and if the case warrants it, seek professional assistance. It may take some work but believe that God will reward your efforts and the results in your relationship with your children as well as the legacy you will leave.

Damaging words are not always angry ones. Sometimes just the tone used can be equally as destructive. As fathers, we have the charge of bringing up our children to be strong and confident members of society and that is severely damaged when we undercut the child's self-esteem through the use of demeaning and debasing verbiage. When it comes to being condescending, it is important to understand that condescending language is no better than angry verbal insults. This is because condescension is ultimately pride in spoken form. When a father condescends to his children, he is letting them know that despite the fact that they are his children (or step-children), he holds them in a lower regard as if they are not up to his level.

This often (but not always) goes hand-in-hand with fathers who are quick to criticize and nitpick their children while being extremely slow to offer praise and encouragement. Reasons for this can be many, ranging from an unreasonably high level of expectation to a cycle of upbringing where the father endured a similar childhood and in turn knows no better in dealing with his own children. Please realize that the pressure we place upon our children, although well meant, can lead to resentment. God does not force or pressure anybody into anything, but He gently calls us into a relationship with Him. He does not criticize us when we make mistakes but He does convict us when we step out of His will and He offers us a way back to the right path if we accept His correction and look for it.

There is an expression that says it takes ninety-nine compliments to erase one critical comment. If this is true, many of us will have to spend the rest of our lives providing compliments to make up for the things that we have said out of our feelings and emotions. The Bible instructs fathers not to embitter their children if they wish to establish a positive relationship with their child. Our words have power therefore, we must offer praise and encouragement to our children as often as possible. In doing so, we begin to build on a solid foundation and so in times of correction, the children will not feel discouraged or embittered. They will realize that for better or worse, they are loved by their earthly father which hopefully translates to them knowing that they are loved similarly by the Father.

Stinging words of criticism can hurt but a father who is passive aggressive and carries equally passive aggressive body language. Passive aggressiveness can be defined as someone who retaliates in a subtle way rather than speaking his mind. For some fathers, especially the ones who are non-confrontational, this is one major avenue commonly used. The paths of passive aggressiveness can range from being a distant and inefficient father to being reluctant to indulge or accept suggestions from others in the family to resenting and blaming others for things that have happened in his life. Whatever the issue, the effect is the same—the family suffers from our malcontent. It is important that body language, while it can be misunderstood, is usually a means to express feelings that may not be spoken This means of communication sometimes speaks louder than words. As people it is easy to manipulate the words that we speak and formulate a false personality. However, body language is much more difficult to fake since some of our body language is expressed subconsciously.

This is one issue that has been a big thing for me personally. Whenever I am irritated with anyone, I usually will not say much but my body language speaks volumes to my displeasure. In the Bible, Jesus speaks on knowing people by their fruits. In Matthew, He speaks in regards to false prophets, but this can also relate to men who are to be fathers who don't need to show body language that shows displeasure and serves as a shell for harboring resentment. Jesus said in Matthew 7:15-20, "You will know them by their fruits" (NKJV). It was so important that Jesus mentioned it twice! Fathers need to understand that children will almost always follow the actions of a father. A father's actions must be loving, clear, and most importantly, godly. If we hope to escape and avoid the pitfalls of being labeled abusive, we must put in the work. Just as God does not abuse us, we should not deal harshly with the children that He has given us. God is love and we are to exude just that, with every fiber of our being.

Part Two: The Collapse of Fatherhood

THE PASSIVE FATHER

—

Traditionally in many parts of the world, men go to work and make the money to support the family while the woman takes care of the children and the home. As times have changed and more women are following their ambitions and have more opportunities to do so there are many men who have not made the adjustment to balance the household by taking more of a responsibility in the home with the raising of the children and being active in their daily upbringing. This is not meant to criticize fathers for wanting to provide for their children, it is a simple matter of addressing the fact that as more women work and have careers, fathers also need to balance the household by helping out more with the children and doing other things to make the home run more smoothly.

One thing that some fathers tend to do is to delegate responsibilities to others while attending to personal affairs. His intentions may be noble, but the responsibility of every father to raise and mentor his children remains the same. Fathers, this is said with love and respect: it is not the responsibility of the school, the pastor, the youth group, the babysitter, the coach, the media, or any other outlet to raise the children that have been put in your charge. Whether you are fighting against time or not, our involvement in the development of our children is essential.

Passiveness in a father very rarely leads to development. It only leads to a loss of relationship. A passive father cannot lead his family. He ultimately sets a bad example for his sons and a low standard for his daughters as they grow up. Passive fatherhood is wrong, dangerous, and must be repented of.

When we were lost in our sins, God did not send an angel or someone else to redeem mankind. Instead, He Himself stepped into history to do it in the form of Jesus Christ. He healed people and delivered them from their infirmities. It was also His hands that bore the nails of the cross on Calvary and it was His blood that was spilled as a sacrifice for our redemption. It was Jesus who took the keys of death and hell from the devil. It was, it is, and it always will be Jesus—our advocate. Looking at the life of Jesus, He set the example for us to follow. He was not passive in His teachings or communication. He set out the perfect example to follow. Now, imagine if Jesus would have been passive in his love and care for us. We would not have the gift to come before God and be heard and forgiven. Thankfully, Jesus knew better. Just as Jesus redeemed, loved, and cared, we should too with our children.

In conjunction with the passive, hands-off fathering some men engage in, there are some who take it even further. They not only turn a blind eye, but also let their children stumble and fall without any guidance. Granted, a father should provide room for the growth of their child, but never free range to derail into sin and darkness. Allowing children to grow and do whatever they want is not love, it is a recipe for a disastrous life for the children and heartache for the father who allows it to happen. One result of choosing to allow the children to do as they please is an eventual loss of respect for the father and an ultimate loss of respect for any authority figure which includes:

teachers, coaches, and even law enforcement. King Solomon addresses children in several verses, where he urges them in several instances such as in Proverbs 10:17, "The one who follows instruction is on the path to life, but the one who rejects correction goes astray" (Holman) and again in Proverbs 19:20, "Listen to counsel and accept discipline, that you may be wise the rest of your days" (NASB). In order for a child to accept instruction, instruction must first be given.

ALLOWING OUR CHILDREN TO DO WHATEVER THEY WANT AND BEHAVE HOWEVER AS THEY PLEASE WITHOUT GUIDANCE IS NOT PARENTING. IT IS ONE WAY IN WHICH WE CAN FAIL IN RAISING THEM.

God does not expect us to live a holy life without instruction. It is for this reason that the entire Bible was given to mankind and for those who do not believe it is so, look at the world that chooses to live outside of God's instruction. It is plain to see that such a world is chaotic and it is the ultimate reason that there are so many problems in this world. God, like the fathers He has called us to be, provides instruction but He will not force us to listen or adhere to the instruction He gives. In this way, no man can point a finger at God and blame Him for their difficulties. He has done His part and now, He waits on us to do ours. In the same way, we need to provide proper instruction to our children to ensure that they have the best possible chance at a long and prosperous life. Wisdom comes from listening to counsel and without it children are like a person walking in the dark with no light to guide them.

Sooner or later, they will trip and fall. Fathers need to live in godly instruction and provide godly instruction. Actions speak louder than words, don't let hypocrisy seep into fatherhood.

Passiveness cannot coexist with fatherhood. Children need fatherly advice, comfort, and support as they navigate their way through life. This might mean that sometimes a good father will have to actively step into wavering waters for their child. Whether the child may need physical, mental, spiritual, or emotional support, the father must be present to navigate the waters with them. A father must protect their child at all costs. Do not sit back and watch your child drown in the ocean of pain, uncertainty, and worry. It is our responsibility to provide wise counsel and diligent guidance.

In the Bible, God saw that all people on the planet were in trouble after He created mankind and mankind fell into sin through disobedience. Over several centuries God sent prophets, messengers and even enemies to try to get people to turn back to Him but His people were stiff-necked and stubborn. Finally, God sent his son Jesus Christ to secure redemption and salvation. One thing to note however is that when Jesus was on the earth, He was very active in the lives of the people He interacted with on a daily basis. There is never a time in the Bible where Jesus saw people in need and did nothing to help. Instead, everywhere He went He did good things for people. Jesus once explained His mission on earth in John 6:38, "For I have come down from heaven not to do my will but to do the will of Him who sent me." He then followed this saying in John 14:9, when He explained who He was when He proclaimed, "Anyone who has seen Me has seen the Father" (NLT).

Jesus is the perfect example of God the Father and as Jesus was not passive, God the Father is not passive. Hence, since we have been created in the image of God, we too should not be passive. As followers of Christ and fathers or future fathers, we cannot sit on the sidelines. When Eve was tempted by the serpent in the Garden of Eden, Adam was passive and did not intervene. As a result, Eve was deceived and disobeyed God. Worse yet, Adam joined her in disobedience and they were punished. Since then, the world has suffered through their disobedience. Passiveness is not victimless and when a father is passive, he is not only affecting his child but his children's children. The time is now to put passiveness aside and fully clothe yourselves in the armor of God. Your children need you your legacy needs it, future generations need it—let us not let them down.

REVIEW & ANALYSIS

Take some time to review this section. Whether you are by yourself or in a group, be honest with yourself about the following questions:

- Are there any of these topics we have discussed (or others) that may apply to you? In what way(s)?
- Why do you think that you may deal with any of these issues?
- Do you think that these issues can affect your relationship or any legacy you may leave behind? How?
- Do you think that any of these struggles are justifiable? Why or why not?
- What changes (be honest and realistic) do you plan to make to address your assessment of yourself and any sincere shortcomings you may have admitted to dealing with?

Part Three:

DO YOUR FATHERLY DUTY

Part Three: Do Your Fatherly Duty

THE DUTIES OF A FATHER

—

As we have gone through the very exhaustive list of failures that fathers tend to face, it is easy to become discouraged and wonder what comes next. We may wonder, "Can this be fixed?" or "Can I be the father that my children need?" The answer is YES! As mentioned before, knowledge of our failures is one big step but this alone is not enough. In order to improve, fathers need to know what our roles in the family are.

—

ANY MALE CAN MAKE BABIES BUT IT TAKES A TRUE MAN TO BE A GOOD FATHER.

—

By knowing and understanding what we should do as men and fathers, it makes fatherhood more focused so that we can spend our energy doing that which will grow into a lasting and godly legacy. Any male can make babies but it takes a true man to be a good father. What makes the difference? A father does what he needs to do in order to raise his children well in an environment that fosters their development internally and externally.

Part Three: Do Your Fatherly Duty

PROTECTOR

—

Throughout this book the main point that has been echoed repeatedly is that each and every father has a calling and a duty towards his children. No man is excused and no man is exempt within the limits of his abilities but there are some who fall short because they are unsure of what those duties may be. There is no how-to manual on fatherhood (or motherhood) and with the Lord's help and the guidance of the Bible, the Holy Spirit, and the wisdom of generations of our own fathers and grandfathers, each father has to take his own unique steps. There are however certain expectations and duties that each father must fulfill in order to do right by his children and ensure a godly example to follow.

A father who is worthy of esteem and admiration is one who protects his family. To be clear, protection is defined as a conscious effort "to defend or guard from attack, invasion, loss, annoyance, insult, or to cover or shield from injury or danger." Sometimes the protection that is needed from a father is physical. When a child is in a threatening, aggressive, or perilous situation it is the duty of the father to step in and intervene in whatever measure is needed to ensure that his children do not get hurt.

Note that to be a godly father, a man cannot be selfish but must be willing to sacrifice for the sake of his children. Physical protection can range anywhere from holding a scared child at night to confronting a bully or contending with someone who tries to break into your home, or dealing with people who do not have your children's best interest at heart. In short, a father does what he needs to do in order to make the safety of his family one of his highest priorities. I know that in the time I have been a father, I have had to confront other people who have tried to pick on my children because they were younger or smaller or different than others. I have also had to deal with teachers who I did not believe were looking out for the best interests of my children. I do not say this to shame anyone or to brag on myself but simply to demonstrate that every one of us will face this duty in one way or another and we will need to be prepared if we are to succeed.

When we protect our children, we are not looking at being threatening and we do not provide an aura of intimidation. It means however, that we are tender when we need to be tender and tough when we need to be tough but in the context of the overall good and safety of our children. Jesus continually set this example for us throughout His earthly ministry as we read throughout the New Testament, Jesus was tender with the women, children, and the humble but He was tough with the pharisees and those who looked to tread on others. He was very approachable and people occasionally fought to get to Him, He invited children to come to Him, He did not tolerate those who looked to hurt others. He was a protector and we need to be like that. Approachable by our children but ready to confront issues that arise in their lives. Let us work to be more like Jesus.

In addition to that which is seen, we need to offer protection for that which is not, through regular prayer for our children. The Apostle Paul spoke to this very issue when he taught his lessons regarding spiritual warfare which whether you believe in the spirit world or not, is a very real and active thing. In Ephesians 6:11-12, Paul spoke to the struggle of the war that is unseen in the verse where he states, "Wear the full armor of God. Wear God's armor so that you can fight against the devil's clever tricks. Our fight is not against people on earth. We are fighting against the rulers and authorities and the powers of this world's darkness. We are fighting against the spiritual powers of evil in the heavenly places" (ERV).

Fathers, take note that while things can sometimes appear to be calm on the surface, especially when children are in their adolescent and young adult years, it is not always the case underneath the surface and treading carelessly can lead to dire consequences. The devil wants your children and he would love to destroy them at every level possible and as a father, it is your duty, and your honor, to fight for and defend them by the power of the Holy Spirit. Now it is important to note that this scripture applies to everyone. No one is immune to the attacks of the enemy however in the same way that we would not sit by and watch our children get beaten up physically or verbally, we apply this scripture in the spiritual warfare we are in. When we do not pray for, and with, our children we are can leave them vulnerable to spiritual harm. May we never let this happen on our watch.

In reality, there are a lot of fathers both in today's society and in the past, who suffer from a lackadaisical attitude which sometimes translates to a lack of awareness for what is happening. Some do not realize it but they are in a serious spiritual battle for a child's heart and mind.

There are some parents (mothers and fathers) who hand this responsibility to others to do the fighting or, in some cases, they leave the child to fight and fend for themselves often with spiritual, and sometimes physical consequences. This is a major reality in the lives of many children across the globe. Every single day of the year, children are pressured on all sides and have to struggle with everything from pornography and sex, fitting in with peers, dealing with physical and social issues, and cyber bullying to experimenting with and abusing drugs. All in all, it is best to safeguard children through prayer. We must stay vigilant and do everything possible so that our children can thrive in all their endeavors.

> **AS FATHERS, WE NEED TO PUT ON THE WHOLE ARMOR OF GOD AND BE PREPARED TO FIGHT FOR OUR CHILDREN ON A DAILY BASIS.**

By putting on the whole armor of God, every father makes sure that he is ready for battle at all times. All fathers need to be men of valor, who will fight for their children. There is no more time for fainthearted or cowardly men who dedicate their efforts more on watching or playing sports, video games, other hobbies, or pursuing career goals that leave the family exposed. These things aren't bad in and of themselves but they need to be prioritized. Children need fathers to be a source of strength and a beacon in darkness. It is time for fathers everywhere to step up and take responsibility for looking after the well-being of our children—no excuses.

The armor of God is something we are all called to wear every day. It includes the helmet of salvation, the breastplate of righteousness, the shield of faith, the belt of truth, the sword of the spirit, and the shoes of the gospel. The one place where there is no protection is the back, because God expects us to stand and fight not turn and run. In Spartan culture, a soldier could face the death penalty for fleeing from a conflict because it broke Spartan code of "No retreat, no surrender." Each man fought with honor and bravery. They always gave sacrificially to protect their people and their land. This is the very dedication a real father needs to have towards being a protector. While we don't need to be aggressive or combative in our demeanor, we must make sure that we are ready to defend our children. We must never give up and never surrender. Our children's lives depend on us.

It is important to understand that this is no joke or laughing matter. The devil hates the God ordained establishment of family. The devil will do anything and everything to distort what God loves. Consequently, each father needs to make sure that he partners with the Lord day in and day out to ensure that his family is covered in prayer and protected spiritually and physically. Whether you believe it or not, there are spiritual forces that are at work in each and every family. A lot of the fighting is done on our knees as we pray to the Lord and spend time with Him both individually and as a family. The duty to protect is non-negotiable and it is something we have to do regularly and with tenacity. We protect that which we love and if we love our children, we will protect them.

God is known as a protector for all of His children and there are many Christians across the world who can attest to the fact that Jesus is known as our Shepherd. In the book of Psalm, David refers to God as a protector in many instances notably in Psalm 18:2 in which David states, "The Lord is my protector; he is my strong fortress. My God is my protection, and with Him I am safe. He protects me like a shield; He defends me and keeps me safe" (NLT). He also references God's protection in the most famously known chapter in the Bible, Psalm 23 where David begins by calling God his shepherd. Throughout the chapter, David details how God takes care of him and protects him from dangers left and right. In the New Testament, Jesus refers to God the Father as a protector in John 17:12, "While I was with them, I kept them safe. I kept them safe by the power of your name—the name you gave me. I protected them. And only one of them was lost—the man (Judas) that chose to be lost. He was lost so that what was said in the Scriptures would happen" (NLT). As a note to all fathers, God protects us as His own and we should do the same for ours. It is our God-given duty.

When a man takes the time to pray for his children, he is setting the example of how important time with the Lord is and also how important the safety of his children is to him. He, essentially, stands as a God-appointed guard over his family acting in the authority of Jesus Christ, as a sentry against the schemes at attacks of the devil. A father who does not have caution in matters like these is often passive and silent but a father who truly does will fight whether it be in the physical or spiritual to make sure that his children are protected and secure.

Part Three: Do Your Fatherly Duty

PROVIDER

—

Besides protecting his family, a father has the duty to provide for his children. As mentioned earlier in the book, Paul addresses this issue in 1 Timothy 5:8 where he states that a man who does not provide for his household has denied the faith and is worse than an unbeliever. This shows just how serious God is about this duty that He has placed with every father. Being called an unbeliever ultimately means that you do not belong to Christ and this is even worse than someone who truly does not know Christ. The reason for this is because some men know the truth and they know God's expectation but they knowingly choose to go on their own path. Such people should not expect to receive much from the Lord until they turn back to God and repent of selfish ways. Despite the shift in societal norms and the surge of women who have become very successful in the workplace, a fully-abled man should never allow his wife to pay his way while calling himself a follower of Christ. While we must honorably celebrate, encourage, and share the accomplishments and successes of women in the workplace, a man should lead his family and not depend solely on his wife or children for financial stability.

The Apostle Paul writes in Ephesians 4:28, "Let the thief no longer steal, but rather let him labor, doing honest work with his own hands, so that he may have something to share with anyone in need" (ESV). Please note that Paul does not mention that a father should be picky about the job he has but he should have an honest job where he can provide for his children's needs. There are many men who, while working towards their dreams and callings, work in jobs that they might not necessarily prefer but they do it in service to the Lord and for the benefit of their children. Some men however tend to pass up job after job claiming to be waiting for the perfect job opportunity all the while relying on others to fulfill the role that he was meant for.

A MAN WHO DOES NOT PROVIDE FOR HIS FAMILY IS WORSE THAN UNBELIEVER.

One main complaint that I have heard from several friends of mine who just happen to be single mothers relate to this very issue: most of the financial responsibility is laid solely upon them to find a way to provide for their children while some the fathers do not have jobs that live up to their potential and seemingly have no ambition or they do not work at all and the do contribute very little or not at all financially. Whether the parents are together or not, a man is to always find a way to provide for his children. Sporadic gifts and pat on the backs are not enough. We can all stand to do more.

When a fully capable man chooses not to work and provide for his children, it has a detrimental effect that can ripple down to his children and the way that they think. This kind of behavior, besides being irresponsible, has a tendency to demonstrate that family is not a priority. Paul's expression of such a man being an unbeliever is a stinging rebuke as the heart of such a father is focused on misguided or selfish motives. Selfishness is totally against the nature of God, instead we are to live lives of service to one another and sacrifice for others. This is the definition of true love.

God is a provider for all of us who call Him Father. Paul stated in Philippians 4:19 "And God shall supply all your needs according to His riches in glory by Christ Jesus". Now this does not provide a license for laziness but it does mean that God will crown our efforts with success when it lines up with His will. We need to make sure that we walk in the confidence of this promise and do all that we can do to make sure we are doing our part to provide. This is what it means to walk hand-in-hand with the Father who has called us to fulfill this sacred duty.

SPORADIC PAYMENTS AND PATS ON THE BACK ARE NOT ENOUGH WHEN IT COMES TO PROVISION FOR OUR CHILDREN.

As we provide for our children, we need to teach our children the benefits of hard and honest work. We need to show them what it means to develop character and integrity through the process of working the way up the ladder. As I have emphasized a few times, children will watch to see if what you say and what you do match and they will almost always go with what you do over what you say. A father should live the advice he gives to his children through his everyday living. In the words of D.L. Moody,

"A man ought to live so that everybody knows he is a Christian…and mostly his family ought to know." As Christians we follow the example of Jesus Christ who showed the nature of God and He lived each lesson that He taught but even for those who do not yet know Jesus, it is encouraged to read through the Bible and see that Jesus demonstrated (and continues to demonstrate) the very things he has required of us. Even when they were hard and not the most popular things to do or say. In the same way, we need to do what is right and integral even when it is difficult, inconvenient, or requires sacrifice. Providing for our children, like protecting them, shows that we love and care about them. Most of us love our children and we can give without loving but we cannot love without giving. As God so loved the world that He gave the best, we should love our children so much that we too are willing to give all that we can for their good.

Part Three: Do Your Fatherly Duty

GUIDE

—

The duties of any father are like a three-legged stool. He is to protect his family sacrificially, he is to provide for his family by doing whatever he needs to do within the constraints of the law, performing honest work and bringing home a paycheck. The duty of providing guidance to his children is the third leg of fatherhood. A true father provides his children with the tools to survive the journey of life which we know can get difficult at times. In order to achieve this, a father needs to provide advice or information on how to resolve problems or navigate difficult situations. Being an authority figure plays a very big part into the way that guidance is received and processed by the children. During childhood, guidance should be very hands-on and direct. As the child grows older guidance can be more verbal where a child has to make decisions for himself or herself, but one thing remains constant through it all- the guidance of a father. As I mentioned earlier, my children will often come to me to ask for help or ask a question about something.

As they get older and more independent, they may ask less for my help and more for my advice even though I don't believe that it will ever stop completely. As their father, it is my duty to guide them in godly living and good decision making as long as I am alive. In my opinion if we raise our children with the rules of what is acceptable in society and what is not, why not do the added work to raise them to love and trust in God to keep and bless their lives?

The Bible is God's guidance to us in the fact that God teaches through history and we can learn lessons from others who obeyed and others who disobeyed His commands and precepts. After His death, resurrection, and ascension, Jesus gave us the Holy Spirit who serves many purposes, one of which is to guide us in all truth. Jesus ultimately encouraged believers that He would never leave or forsake them and He still offers guidance and comfort whenever needed to those who listen for it. In the same way, a father cannot force a child to adhere to his guidance but it is his responsibility to offer it and to let his children know that he is always there to support them.

Another area that every father is to provide guidance for his children is on a spiritual front. As previously mentioned, the devil's primary purpose is to destroy the family and he will do whatever he can to make this happen. Whether it is in the physical or the spiritual realm, many of the things that happen have a correlation and connection with each other. This means that things that are not protected in the spiritual can be attacked and affected in the physical. In Luke 22: 31-34, Jesus spoke to Peter saying, "Simon, Simon, Satan has asked to sift all of you as wheat. But I have prayed for you, Simon that your faith may not fail. And when you have turned back, strengthen your brothers." Jesus explains here that the devil has plans for us just as the Father has plans for us. However, the devil looks to destroy us systematically, methodically, and completely while Jesus has assured us that He has come to give life and give it more abundantly (John 10:10).

Fathers need to pray for their children regularly and without fail because prayer moves the hand of God and prayer is how we communicate with God when looking for guidance. We can then take what God tells us or the various lessons we have learned in life and pass that knowledge down to our children. Advice and guidance are like building blocks and if we want our children to stand firm, they will need something solid to stand on and nothing is more solid than that which comes from the hand and the Spirit of God.

It is no secret that a child will often imitate a parent and as they grow it will stick with them in some regard. It is important for children to see you go to church, to see you pray, and to see you read your Bible and worship God. This shows them just how important it is to you and how much it means to spend time with God. It is never too late to start raising the next generation up in the ways of the Lord. Family leadership should not be left to any other individual. I will say it again, this is your duty and it needs to be taken seriously. Do what you have to do to leave a godly legacy. It may not always be easy or convenient but it is always worth it.

It is very important to remember that being a parent is one of the biggest blessings a person can have in life. As with anything worth having, there is work that will be required and it won't always be easy but there is little that could ever substitute it. This book tends to address areas of shortcomings that we may encounter or struggle with as fathers but the good news is that we can overcome it if we are willing to put in the work and dedication. We can make progress and thrive as godly men and fathers and we can make sure that we enjoy this charge that God has placed in our hands. The upbringing of a child is a daily routine and it requires day-to-day leadership because being a father is a daily job.

> **GUIDANCE GOES BEYOND HAVING ALL OF THE ANSWERS. IT MEANS WORKING TOGETHER WITH OUR CHILDREN TO FIND ANSWERS.**

This is often where many of us miss the mark because as many of us wane in the undertaking of household responsibilities, the women oftentimes end up picking up the slack left behind and this many times, includes the everyday upbringing of the children. The Lord Jesus demonstrated time and time again, that leadership is often done through serving others. In Matthew 20:28 and Mark 10:45, Jesus clarified His mission when He stated that, "the Son of Man did not come to be served, but to serve, and to give his life as a ransom for many." Fathers are called to lead and that is done through offering guidance and performing service to the family as Jesus does and while it might not involve the washing of feet, service comes in many other ways such as cooking, laundry, being there when a child falls ill, helping them with schoolwork wherever needed, and guiding our children by listening to them and being a part of the lives. Note one important thing, guidance goes beyond having all the answers. Guidance sometimes means that we work together with our children where we can use our life experiences to help our children find answers to life's questions. If you can be of help you can serve. The question is, "Will you?"

Fathers, each day is a war whether it is in the physical or the spiritual and the duty falls to each father, with the guidance and governance of the Lord, to lead his family in prayer. As we pray for the glory of God to be displayed in our homes, we have to be sure to speak the blessings and the protection of God over our children as they sleep, as they go out and come home, and as they grow from year to year. In Proverbs 18:21 the Bible states, "The tongue can speak words that bring life or death. Those who love to talk must be ready to accept what it brings" (ERV) and where a father chooses the former in speaking words that bring life, he speaks the very thing that God wants for each and every one of us. This means abstaining from cruel, demeaning and criticizing words or actions as this can bring emotional, spiritual, and even physical harm to his children. A father's legacy can be one of building up or tearing down but it all starts with building the words that are spoken and the daily life that follows. Both of these determine how much guidance a child will receive, accept, and implement into his or her own life. Being successful in the effort to guide the children will ensure that their spiritual and physical lives are being addressed and a godly legacy is being established. Therefore, it is important to take this duty seriously and place God at the center of it all.

REVIEW & ANALYSIS

—

Take some time to review this section. Whether you are by yourself or in a group, be honest with yourself about the following questions:

- What does it mean to you to be a good protector, provider, or guide?
- Why do you think that God has called you to these duties?
- Do you feel that you are doing your best to fulfill your duties? Why or why not?
- Where can you look to make some changes or improvements?

Part Four:

ARE YOU FULFILLING YOUR RESPONSIBILITY?

Part Four: Are You Fulfilling Your Responsibility?

THE RESPONSIBILITIES OF A FATHER

—

Some reading this book might ask what the difference is between duty and responsibility? Aren't they the same thing? Duty and responsibility are closely linked but they are not necessarily the same thing. The word 'duty' has been derived from the Latin word 'debere' meaning commitment. When speaking of duty, an individual purposefully, deliberately, and fully commits to it and involves themselves in the activity with no self-interests holding them back or diverting their course. Responsibilities on the other hand are the tasks an individual is solely opting for. Tasks individuals handle and also becomes accountable for the end-result of performing the chosen or given tasks. Responsibility comes with a moral accountability or obligation to get certain things done. Simply put, duty is self-sacrificial, responsibility is obligatory. Additional actions can be implemented as a part of the list of duties but they are both done with the intention of accomplishing a specific goal. Both duty and responsibility are needed. In the last chapter we discussed the former. We will examine the latter in more detail in this segment.

Part Four: Are You Fulfilling Your Responsibility?

NURTURE

—

The first responsibility of a godly father is to raise his children in love and nurture. When something is nurtured, it is cared for, raised up, and encouraged to grow and develop. Children often tend to reflect their environment and if their home environment is turbulent or unstable this instability can become a part of their character. A child's home life will not shape their entire personality but it will definitely affect certain paradigms in regards to their thinking and decision-making which can prove to be very beneficial or detrimental in the long run.

Physical trainers and doctors put a high emphasis on nutrition when it comes to matters of bettering and maintaining one's health. Why? Because when it is neglected it is a matter of time until the body starts to experience problems. This happens because the body does not receive the nurture or nutrients that it needs to function as it should. In this same way we have to provide the nurture that will allow our children and our relationship with our children to thrive. A malnourished relationship will not survive, so we must make sure that all of our children experience the love, care, and discipline that is needed to help them grow in a healthy and godly way. Not only do we need to make sure that our relationships with our children are nourished, we need to them to develop. This is not a one-time thing but an ongoing process that we are largely responsible for maintaining. It is like a garden the needs to be tended and taken care of. If needs to be watered with love and monitored carefully to prevent the growth or development of weeds. A nurturing father does not run a relationship on a one-way street and it is our responsibility to do the best we can to raise nurtured, unspoiled children.

A MALNOURISHED RELATIONSHIP OFTENTIMES WILL NOT SURVIVE.

A father who shows love and nurture ultimately shows the nature of God and the fundamental intentions that He had for fathers to bestow on their children. Nurture is not always hugging and kisses, sometimes it includes discipline and correction whenever a child starts to go astray. Again, it is very important to remember this point: the image we portray is often the image that the children will have of God. The way you handle situations is the way that they believe God handles things and more likely than not they will repeat the cycle with their own children. Be warned that we will reap what we sow. This is true in the decisions we make and it also applies to the legacy that we will leave behind. As an apple seed will begat apples, seeds of violence, anger, or grief will yield the same. Let's aim to make good choices that will help improve our children's' lives.

Nurture and love both take effort and are conscious decisions of the will but as in every successful relationship, they are necessary in order for children to be encouraged in life's journey as well as their spiritual pursuit of godliness. The nurture must take place and the example must be set by each of us who looks to leave a godly legacy with his children. A man who does not lead the way loving the Lord with all their heart, body, and mind cannot hope to expect that of his children.

Part Four: Are You Fulfilling Your Responsibility?

SUCCESS, GRATITUDE, AND HUMILITY

—

In this life every father has been called to ensure that each one of his children grows to be a productive member of society. Success is a unique term because success does not mean the same thing to each person. For some, success is monetary, for some it is fame-based, for others it is based on the accomplishments or dreams achieved but whatever it is, success is something everybody aspires to. Each father plays a role in the level of success (or failure) each child has. For the fathers who are present, giving their children a relationship they can come to, guidance when in doubt, and direction when they are lost, is the ultimate win. To see a child succeed in life is a father's greatest accomplishment. A father honors the Lord when he teaches his children the lessons needed and puts forth the encouragement required to make the push to be successful especially when life pushes back. On the other hand, a father who teaches his children entitlement sets them up for failure but a father who teaches his children the importance of hard work and trusting in the Lord will provide a solid and stable foundation on which they can grow and stand during good and bad times.

I look at my children every day and I think of the hopes, dreams, and prospects I have for them. I also look at the fact that God's plan for them might be different but either way my prayer for them is that they will succeed in life. It is my responsibility to guide them towards successful living as much as I can while nurturing who God has created them to be. This will only happen however if I am fully engaged and involved in their lives, their interests, and their dreams. No man can fulfill his full potential as a father from a distance. I know that if I can fulfill my calling by being an up-close and personable parent, I can leave the rest to the Lord. As fatherhood goes, God will not do our job for us but He will walk with us as we put in a genuine effort to the raising of our children. Take all the encouragement you can. God is pulling for us and our children to succeed and will do His part as we do ours. In Jeremiah 29:11, God makes His intentions clear in one of my favorite verses in the Bible, "For I know the plans I have for you" declares the Lord, "Plans to prosper you and not to harm you, plans to give you hope and a future." We may face challenges but God is for us in every season as we should be for our children.

NO MAN CAN FULFILL HIS FULL POTENTIAL AS A FATHER FROM A DISTANCE.

Some adults of previous generations look at the children of this generation and label them many things: lazy, entitled, ungrateful, and several other negative things to determine a lack of independence. However, this is a stereotype that in many cases, is untrue. Sadly, with the demands and expectations of society today, times can be hard and sometimes a young adult might have to move back in with the parents or other relatives. This should be a temporary situation since it is not okay to choose to remain living with your parents indefinitely, especially if it is done with no intention of contributing or making any progression in life. A father who allows his children to do this is not doing them any favors. The Apostle Paul addresses this issue in the book of 2 Thessalonians chapter 3:10, "For even when we were with you, we gave you this rule: "The one who is unwilling to work shall not eat."

For many fathers, this is the case where they have children who grow up under their roof with few or no responsibilities. For some, they move out and move back in having not matured at all. They expect aging parents to continue to take care of their meals, laundry, housekeeping, and all-around livelihood while they choose to live the life of ease and social ineptitude. They have no plans and refuse to help their parents with maintenance of the household. In cases like this, a father needs to step up and enforce an arrangement in which the child looks to make progress or the child will have to "not eat."

You may think that this line of thinking is meanspirited or coldhearted but at the end of it all you have to ask yourself is, "Who benefits from tough love?" Our children do. Fathers, we are to encourage our children by all means for it is a godly thing to do but do not enable them to become complacent and unmotivated. As the old saying goes, "Idle hands are the devil's workshop." Therefore, fathers must make sure that their children become productive members of society and work as if they are working unto the Lord. This way we as fathers, can be proud in their success and even more importantly, God will be glorified through them.

Supporting and helping your child out is one of the duties and joys of being a father however, allowing them to settle is not and it is not encouraged. Every person is to keep improving and developing, not sinking into complacency.

Being a good father means that sons are taught and consistently reminded of what it means to be godly men and daughters are encouraged to keep working at exceeding their limits, raising their standards, and breaking boundaries. This does not happen if they are not encouraged to become productive members of society. We support them in other ways outside of the home and finances. We should look to help them in achieving their dreams and fulfilling their potential as much as possible.

In conjunction with encouraging their success, we need to ensure that our children learn two valuable lessons: gratitude and humility. Gratitude is the attribute of being thankful with the readiness to show appreciation for something and to return kindness. Humility is a modest or low view of one's own importance. I heard a pastor once say that humility isn't about thinking less of yourself but thinking of yourself less. As we watch our children grow and guide them through the various obstacles of life, we need to show them that all good things come from the Lord and it is by His hand alone that we are uplifted. When we realize that we do not accomplish anything without His help and guidance, it becomes much easier to show gratitude to God for our children and the favor that is given to them when we walk in the ways that God directs us. As I stated before, our children will observe our lifestyle and oftentimes will emulate it in their own lives. This is how a legacy starts and endures through the generations. An attitude of gratitude is something that can be contagious as we need to be eager to pass this among other positive characteristics on to our children. Throughout the

Bible, several authors of the books in the old and new testaments address the need to be grateful and God's perception of gratitude. If the Bible addresses the need to be grateful, I truly believe that it is of paramount importance to take note, incorporate it in our daily living, and show our children that it is a wonderful trait to have, especially if we are to call ourselves Christians and want to leave a godly legacy.

It is also hard, I can imagine, to have a heart of gratitude and a spirit of pride because pride is centered around self-elevation while gratitude often expresses thanks for something that has been done for you by someone else. From a Christian standpoint, we are grateful to God for sending Jesus to die on the cross for our sin and we are called to be humble because we know that without the sacrifice of the cross there is no redemption for any one of us. We know that we cannot save ourselves and we are in need of a savior which is why we call Jesus our Lord and Savior. This principle should apply in our own minds on a daily basis where we teach our children the importance of both but in order for us to demonstrate this quality, we need to practice it in our own lives. How do we encourage this in our legacy? Dou our children see hard work and gratitude for the things we receive in life? Do they see humility in us and the way we speak or do we brag on our accomplishments? Even if you are not a believer, there is no substitute for gratitude and humility because no one wants to raise spoiled and ungrateful children.

God has given us the opportunity to be fathers and we should always be humble that whether we believe we are good fathers or not, every day is a chance to be better than the day before. When we adopt this mindset and incorporate it into the way that we live, our children will be able to see that we are not an entity unto ourselves and despite what society may say, no man is an island. No man does it all by himself.

It teaches that there is no reason to feel shame in asking for help and accepting it whenever it is made available. God makes note of our attitudes and our children always look to see not just what we do but our approaches and mindsets towards the various circumstances we face

> GRATITUDE AND HUMILITY GO HAND IN HAND. GOD SEES OUR ATTITUDES WHILE OUR CHILDREN SEE OUR APPROACH AND MINDSET.

in life. Let us make good on our legacy by ensuring that we do it with gratitude and humility. We need to put into perspective that we are not better than anyone else, we are blessed by God. We need to remember this and remind our children that gratitude and humility are godly traits and they lead to fulfilling and meaningful lives.

Part Four: Are You Fulfilling Your Responsibility?

HONESTY & AVAILABILITY

—

In today's world, people are so busy and so focused on self that we place limits on our availability. As a result, others tend to slip through the cracks and are made to feel less important than God would want them to feel. I hope to make this extremely clear and I say this in all love and respect to everyone reading this book. The only thing that leaves this earth after death are the souls of people. Nothing else really matters and it is important to remember that Jesus came, lived, died, and rose for people and Jesus calls us to reach out to people as well. This does not happen if people make themselves unavailable to others. This applies also to how much of a priority people are in our lives. If we become too busy for others our children will most likely follow in our footsteps. Fathers (and mothers who may be reading) please make time for your children. As I stated in part two, fathers are needed to be present in the home. Fatherhood is 24 hours a day, 365 days a year. It does not have office hours and it is not a 9-to-5 schedule. Nothing in the world is more important than the relationship and the legacy we will leave with them. If your legacy shows a lack of availability and accessibility, there will be a cycle that forms with the children where they may do the same and may think that God is like that as well. This cannot be further from the truth but it is much easier to believe if children see godly attributes in us as their parents. Just imagine that which you do to your children could be passed down to your grandchildren. Is it something that you would be proud of or something that would bring humiliation and regret? Would you say that you represented God well or not? Think on it and make the necessary adjustments.

FATHERHOOD DOES NOT HAVE OFFICE HOURS. IT IS NOT LIKE A 9-TO-5 JOB.

We need to ensure that we are honest and open to discussion. In the part two, the subject of an authoritarian father who speaks but does not listen was addressed. In conjunction to accessibility and availability, an honest and open discussion between a father and his children usually tends to strengthen a bond between them. Priority is felt and learned, and children only learn and reciprocate if we give them just that. This comes through knowing that any communication between the two will be a well-defined two-way street where both the father and the child will be able to work on understanding one another's point of view. Even if the father ultimately has a different point of view, a child can feel like he/she has gotten to speak their mind and they have been heard thus making it more likely that they will be willing to speak openly and honestly. Making ourselves available may be hard sometimes but it is a responsibility we must make a priority if we hope to raise our children well. We wont get more out of a relationship than we are willing to put into it so let us put the effort into setting up the legacy that we hope to be remembered for.

Spiritually, when a Christian speaks to God through prayer, God listens and answers openly and honestly. In 1 Peter 5: 7, Peter said, "Give all your worries to him, because he cares for you" (ERV). What did Peter mean by this simple but powerful verse? It means that Christians should not worry or be afraid to speak honestly to God about the things in our lives. God will most definitely answer any prayer made with a genuine heart. It is very important to note however that God will also be honest with you and while He will not always take your side He is always on your side as His child because He wants the best for each one of us. God is honest, He is righteous, He is available 24/7, and He will always look to steer us with love, in the right direction. Fathers need to be like this with their own children and by following the examples set and learn from the mistakes made through the Bible. It isn't always easy but it can be done. Just imagine if God did not care. How many of us would actually pray or care to know anything about God at all? It wouldn't be a very good relationship would it? But God, in His wisdom, listens with patience and answers our prayer at the perfect time—His time.

As in any conversation, there is a balance of speaking and listening and it is of utmost importance to maintain such a balance in order for good and honest communication between a father and his children to be maintained. It is also very important to have a good balance between our verbal and physical reaction. This usually involves taking some time to listen, think, process, then react accordingly. When a father processes before reacting, it gives him the opportunity to weigh the information and act in the most appropriate manner. A lifestyle of this kind of behavior sets up a legacy that testifies that honesty and open conversation are necessary and very advantageous to lasting relationships.

The timeless saying goes, "think before you speak" and this simple truth carries far and wide in the rearing and the raising of children. Without a good balance of availability and honesty, no relationship will grow and will eventually begin to rot and decay into nothingness. This is the last thing that we should desire for ourselves or our children.

It is important to note that our honesty and availability can have lasting physical and spiritual consequences and every father will be held responsible by God for his role and his words (or lack thereof). Many times, when our children see that we are neither honest or available to them or we never seem to be satisfied with them or encouraging to them, they have the potential to shut us out or give up on us. When a child gives up on their father (yes it does happen if we are being completely honest) it is a major breach in the relationship because when a child gives up on their father, they no longer feel the need or desire to grow close to them. At this point our children let go of us and we then need to do the majority of the work to repairing the relationship we broke by our lack of encouragement, support, transparency or accessibility. This does not need to be and, if we want to be the leaders of our homes like we have been called to be, we cannot shirk this responsibility.

WITHOUT A GOOD BALANCE OF COMMUNICATION, NO RELATIONSHIP WILL GROW.

Every father must learn to use his two ears and one mouth in that order and he needs to ensure that his comments and actions ultimately uplift his children even when they make mistakes and missteps in life, even when correction is necessary. God shows this example throughout the Bible when dealing with the Israelites who fell away from Him time after time and yet, like the loving father that He is, God picked them up, brushed them off, and worked to restore them and point them in the right direction. Despite their many failures, God maintained his availability to them as He does with His children today. This is what He expects of every father when dealing with his children in order to build and strengthen lives and relationships while reflecting the plan He has had for every family since the very beginning. Honesty and availability are two bedrock responsibilities for every one of us. Let us make sure we have a good foundation to build on.

Part Four: Are You Fulfilling Your Responsibility?

SETTING (OR RESETTING) A LEGACY

—

Every father has the responsibility to set a legacy that is honoring God and man in that order. In the Old Testament, Joshua, the protégé of Moses who delivered the Israelites out of Egypt, spoke to the people after Moses' death and spoke plainly to the Israelites in Joshua 24:15, where he gave his people a choice to do what is needed when he made the declaration, "But maybe you don't want to serve the LORD. You must choose for yourselves today. Today you must decide who you will serve. Will you serve the gods that your ancestors worshiped when they lived on the other side of the Euphrates River? Or will you serve the gods of the Amorites who lived in this land? You must choose for yourselves. But as for me and my family, we will serve the LORD" (ERV). In this verse, Joshua planted his flag in the sand and proclaimed where his legacy would stand. It didn't mean that he wouldn't have to work for it but his eyes, his focus, and his determination for his family's legacy were all aligned and set in one direction. Jesus reiterated this clearly as he taught in Matthew 6:33, "But seek first the kingdom of God and his righteousness, and all these things will be added to you" (ESV).

In both the Old and the New Testaments, one thing is clear and consistent: the devotion and service first and foremost to God. A father who teaches his children to honor both God and man will set his children up for physical and spiritual success.

A person can honor man and not God but a person cannot honor God and not honor man accordingly. This is not to say that man and God deserve the same kind of honor because God deserves all the honor for who He is and what He has done. God is the one who is in control and He alone deserves to be praised but that does not mean that we cannot show respect to our teachers, employers, bosses, pastors, coaches, or anyone else who is in a position of authority over us. Setting the example of such a thing teaches the way that children should grow thus setting the legacy that shows that we are to give honor where honor is due, all to the glory of the Lord God.

Aside from that, the legacy of a father being a man, being present and involved shows that his family is important and has immense value to him. This sets up part of our legacy as our children grow to see that they are loved. Through unconditional love, accessibility, and discipline (not abuse), a legacy can be established. Being present and involved also demonstrates one of God's biggest traits and fulfills one of His biggest promises to always be there for us. This is sometimes done through us as we raise our children and instill the values to build them up. This is one of the other reasons why we are to make sure that our legacy is a godly one. God uses us to reach the next generation in the everyday lives that they live. He uses our hands, minds, and words to do His will so we have to take it seriously. It is important to remember that whether we are there or not, we are going to leave a legacy that will last. Why not make the time, effort, and enjoy fatherhood while leaving a fruitful legacy?

We have read about several responsibilities that we are to fulfill each and every day, I would suggest if you have had any thoughts or God has spoken to your heart about your responsibilities, that you write them down as soon as possible. We don't want you to forget or for the enemy to steal whatever God has planted in your heart. The main thing that we need to keep in our minds is that our children will grow and develop based on how seriously we take our responsibility. We are to ensure that our relationship with our children is nurtured from the time that they are little and onward. Afterall, our jobs as fathers do not end until our time on earth is done. A nurtured relationship yields children who are successful beyond just money and power. They will grow grateful and humbled by the fact that they had a father who gave them time and love.

GOD USES FATHERS AS INSTRUMENTS THAT HE IS THERE AND HE USES OUR HANDS, MINDS, AND WORDS TO BUILD UP THE NEXT GENERATION IF WE WILL LET HIM USE US.

Like a garden, honesty and availability are like the soil, while our nurture is the fertilizer that we add to the soil. Our advice, character, and godly example serve as the seeds which we plant in the lives of our children. This garden, when tended to properly, yield the fruits of good morals and godly character. Even if you are not a Christian yet, this still applies in the fact that good seed yields good return while neglect oftentimes will yield a poor return. As we follow God's example throughout the Bible, we can show our sons and daughters the promises that He promised to those who listen and in turn, will emulate our legacy (or at least use it as a reference throughout their own lives) for future generations to see. This is our responsibility, our joy, and our charge. As God does His part, we must walk alongside Him and do ours.

Having gone this far in the book there is one last group of fathers that I can think of and I want to assure you that I have not forgotten about you. There are those who may say "I've blown it" or "It's too late, my children are grown" or "My children do not want anything to do with me". Let me encourage you that you are not alone and, as long as you are alive, it is unquestionably possible to reset your legacy regardless of your age or status. It is possible to reset your legacy because it does not hinge solely on the things you have done in the past. If you are trying, honestly, to change there will be obstacles to overcome but the changes you are making will eventually become evident and a change in your family's views and your legacy will slowly begin to form. Rome was not built in a day so do not expect an overnight shift but as you determine to leave a better legacy than the one you started with you are headed in the right direction so do not get discouraged and keep pushing towards a healthier legacy than the one you have set or have had set for you by your ancestors.

In 2 Corinthians 5:17 Paul preached a very important message to a group of people in the city of Corinth; people who had gone off the rails in the way that they were living their daily lives. He said "Therefore, if anyone is in Christ, he is a new creation; old things have passed away; behold all things have become new (NKJV). In his earlier years, Paul's ambition was to imprison and kill Christians whom he saw as radical insurgents to the traditions of the day. After he met Jesus on the way to Damascus to arrest Christians Paul's life changed and he became the author of roughly two-thirds of the New Testament. You may ask, why are you telling me about Paul and what does that have to do with my issues? Paul, changed his legacy and so can you. He did not forget who he was or what he had done (and neither did much of the early church) but he actually owned his faults and shared how Jesus had changed his life and given him a better purpose.

    In the same way, your children might not forget your shortcomings and they may never let you forget it but know that the best thing is to take those lapses in character and use them as stepping stones to being a better man and a better father. You can use your experiences to help steer your children away from making the same mistakes you may have made. In the same way it took the early church to believe that Paul had changed his ways, it may, and probably will, take time for your children to come around but if you are persistent in prayer and practice the outcome will begin to turn in a positive direction. As a tree takes time and care to grow, so does a legacy and the value of your legacy ultimately comes down to the application of several of the things we have discussed as they apply to you and your family dynamic. We are all a work in progress so do not be discouraged if the progress is slow as long as it is moving in the right direction.

REVIEW & ANALYSIS

—

Take some time to review this section. Whether you are by yourself or in a group, be honest with yourself about the following questions:

- What do you think is the difference between your responsibility and your duty as a father?
- How can you nurture, or better nurture, your child to help them grow closer to you in a healthy environment?
- What aspirations and dreams do you have for your children? Are they selfish or selfless in nature? Why or why not?
- What values do you look to instill (or influence) in your children as they grow while still allowing them to develop into who God has created them to be?
- When you feel like you may be deficient as a father, how can you look to be encouraged? What do you think is a good way to stay encouraged?

Part Five:

THE TRUE HEART OF THE FATHER

Part Five: The True Heart of the Father

THE TRUE HEART OF THE FATHER

—

Throughout this book we have discussed several aspects of fatherhood starting with the definition of what fatherhood is to get a clearer picture of what a father is supposed to be. We also discussed several areas in which we tend to fall short because we need to be aware of the areas where we can stand to improve. We then went through the various responsibilities and duties a father is to perform daily. Throughout the book, there have been several references that have been made to God as a Father. For those who are Christians (and even for non-Christians) we learn about God in many respects. But how often do we study Him as more than immortal divinity? God is a father but in respect to fatherhood, who is He really?

All through the Bible, God has been called many things- protector, provider, healer, judge, but many people forget that God is also known by the title of father. It is much easier to see God as an all-powerful being who is up in the heavens looking down on mankind with or without much care (depending on who you are) and not involved in our everyday lives.

You may see God as a sort of genie in the lamp or Santa Claus whose sole purpose is to do what we want, when we want, and how we want it. Thankfully, God is not like Santa Claus that we can think about just once a year or someone who appears at our bidding to do exactly what we want then disappears until the next time we need Him. Whenever the concept of God's fatherhood is rejected or forgotten, a large part of who God is, is overlooked and when God is forgotten, in whole or in part, trouble is undoubtedly soon to follow. In this section we will explore a few aspects of who God is as a father.

Part Five: The True Heart of the Father

HOLINESS

—

Holiness, by definition, means to be specially declared, spiritually pure, and entitled to worship. God is holy by nature and holy in all things that He does. He is the only one who is holy and He is the only one worth of worship. He operates by His Spirit, who the Bible has simply described as the Holy Spirit who lives and operates within every believer. God has called everyone to receive the Holy Spirit but for the sake of this book, He wants fathers to receive and embrace His Holy Spirit wholeheartedly. He wants this for us for a number of reasons, but the overall purpose is that we cannot ever hope to achieve our full potential as fathers without the Holy Spirit's guidance and presence. All men are called to be holy or "dedicated to God" in the way that allows God to shine in the home.

In part three of this book, we discussed that God has called all of us to be protectors, to be providers, and to serve as guides to the next generation through the power of the Holy Spirit. In this section we look at God's holiness and His call to follow in His footsteps. Any other way leads to failure or a short change in the fullness of everything that God has for you as a father and for the children He has given.

He alone is the ultimate example of everything we should strive to be. He is understanding, kind, patient, and when the occasion calls for it, firm and a source of loving discipline. Some may picture God as angry, being ready to rain down fire and brimstone but that cannot be further from the truth. He does things to get our attention when we stray and the choice is ours if we will make a change or continue in our stubbornness. God at His very core is all about love and salvation and He wants to share that with us every day.

It was God the Father who ultimately sent the Son, Jesus Christ, into the world to fulfill the mission of salvation for all mankind. As a father, God has made sure to show nature that He is willing to give everything when He allowed His only begotten son to die in the most horrific and humiliating way. Jesus was arrested, beaten with whips designed to rip flesh to ribbons, spit upon and slapped continually, and ultimately forced to carry a rugged wooden cross through the streets to the outside of the city, where He was stripped naked and nailed. He was then on display for all to see in heaven, on earth, and beneath the earth as God's ultimate plan of salvation was unveiled. There is no salvation without sacrifice and it took the holiness of Jesus for that to happen. There was no other way.

THERE IS NO SALVATION WITHOUT SACRIFICE AND IT TOOK THE HOLINESS OF JESUS FOR THAT TO HAPPEN. THERE WAS NO OTHER WAY.

Why did He do this? John 3:16 makes it very clear that it was purely, totally out of love for each and every person alive now and throughout history. Like the true father that He is, God did not pick and choose who to offer salvation to or the process they would have to follow to get there. When Jesus came, He died and rose for ALL mankind. Not just some but every single person on this earth has been offered the same gift of salvation from a God who is the creator and founder of all things. In Acts 10: 34-35, the Apostle Peter addresses another fatherly quality that some doubt about the goodness of God when he made the proclamation, "I now truly understand that God does not show favoritism, but welcomes those from every nation who fear Him and do what is right" (BSB). Like a good father who does not (and should not) have favorites, God does not favor any race, gender, social, ethnic, or economical group. His love is pure and complete towards each and every person and even though His love is ignored, taken for granted, and even rejected at times, He continues to love and forgive us every day.

Part Five: The True Heart of the Father

LOVE AND SACRIFICE

—

You've probably heard that God is love and it is one of the truest statements ever made. The first and most important action of God's fatherly love is the offering and sacrifice of Jesus Christ. As discussed previously in this book, the crucifixion of Jesus was a sacrifice not just to the physical body of the but it was also to the grief of the Father who watched the sins of all mankind which were placed solely on the shoulders of his perfect Son who stood blameless and was the only worthy and qualified individual to stand in on behalf of sinful man. It was the depth and darkness of the sin of mankind that temporarily separated the perfect union of Father and Son. Jesus was, in that period of time, covered with our sin in order to absolve us of it through the shedding of His blood on Calvary. The blood of Jesus is the one and only thing that can cover our sins and keep us in good standing with the Lord. It is by our acceptance of the sacrifice Jesus made that we can come before God and call Him father. The Father gave what was most precious to Him so that we can also be adopted into the family of God, a family we walk away from when we choose to love sin more than Him.

The sacrifice and resurrection of the Lord Jesus shows that God the Father is wise and caring about His children. God knew that there was a price to pay for sin and mankind as a whole had no way to pay and had ultimately doomed itself to an eternity away from Him in hell. Hell is a place that has been designated simply and purely for the devil and those angels who had fallen in the rebellion plot against God. Through sin and man's choice to embrace sin instead of God, mankind has made the option to join the devil in rebellion against God. As a result, the punishment is the same for mankind. Eternal hell, eternal punishment,

---

JESUS WAS THE ULTIMATE SIGN OF GOD'S LOVE. HIS SACRIFICE WAS THE BIGGEST THING THAT COULD HAVE EVER BEEN GIVEN. NOTHING WILL EVER SURPASS IT.

---

eternal separation from Him but God the Father provided mankind a way out—His name is Jesus. In God's wisdom, He sent Jesus to lay down his life in order to offer each and every person an opportunity to escape punishment. The Apostle Paul made a clear statement of God's love and wisdom towards all of mankind in his letter to the Romans where he wrote, "For the wages of sin is death, but the gift of God is eternal life in Christ Jesus our Lord" (NIV). Just imagine that God's love is so real that He was willing to sacrifice His son so that we could have eternal life with Him. Understand that sin will be paid for one way or another and it can either be paid by the work of Jesus on the cross or it can be paid by the individual through death itself in hell. Sin is so heavy that we can never pay for our sin or the sin of the world, only Jesus can and He will if we ask Him.

Why would God send Jesus to do all of this for us? Why would God choose to have His perfect Son suffer and die for people who would scorn Him, mock Him, disbelieve Him and ultimately reject Him? Why the sacrifice? It was for love and grace. He did it so that no man can say that God is unfair or that He plays favorites. God sent His son so that each and every person can make the decision to personally accept or reject God's offer of eternal life. He wants each and every person to be saved but He will also give us the choice to say no. As the loving father that He is, God will not force anyone to love Him or serve Him instead He will allow us to be prodigals with the hope that we will realize our need for Him and come home.

A good example of this point would be an everyday relationship between a man and wife. In the relationship there is love that should flow between the two but if only one person in the relationship is showing any love, the relationship will not last. Why? Because no one wants to be in a relationship with a person who takes and never reciprocates the love that they receive. On the other hand, nobody wants to be in a relationship where they feel obligated to love the other person. God likewise, does not want us to feel like we are obligated to love Him although He will NEVER stop loving us. Every successful relationship has a balance that involves both parties doing their part. God simply wants us to love Him out of genuine affection. He reaches out in love in every living moment, but the question is will you reach back? God has made His choice and done His part, now it is our turn. A father, likewise, cannot force his children to love him but through the way he lives his life and the legacy he leaves, he can cultivate a home and a relationship with his children where genuine love flows freely—God's ultimate plan.

Love is the epitome of who God is and it is what He is all about but His love is not just about hugs and kisses. Sometimes love can be painful especially during times of trial and correction but it is necessary for growth. Throughout the scriptures, there is no time where God shields His people from disciplinary actions. Instead, God allows us to face the consequences of our actions not to hurt us but to see us grow stronger. An example of this could be a young woman unexpectedly gets pregnant out of wedlock. She may find a relationship with God and repent but that does not mean that the baby disappears or the pregnancy terminates. Rather, God will provide that young mother to-be with the strength to go forward and be the godly mother the child needs as it is born and grows. Another example could be a young man who decides to dabble with drugs or alcohol. When the consequences of such behavior come to fruition, be it police intervention or rehab or anything in between, God does not make those things disappear but He does use those things to systematically help with growth if we are open to it. The sacrifice of Jesus gives us room for repentance and the chance for a do-over. His love allows us to learn and grow from our choices while supporting us in our healing whenever we go astray. That is the Father's true heart.

Part Five: The True Heart of the Father

DISCIPLINE AND PROTECTION

—

Although God is the complete embodiment of love, He does not deliver us from the consequences of sin. He does not abandon us in the midst of it all either. One of Jesus' biggest promises to all Christians is that He will never leave or forsake us whether we feel His presence or not. He allows us to go through various situations in order to allow us to grow into people who depend and trust in Him for everything. In trouble, God never wastes any hardships. He provides avenues for discipline, redemption, and deliverance to restore those who come to Him in humility and genuine repentance. As fathers it is necessary to understand this aspect of God's nature and realize that while it is impossible to shield our children from every difficulty, we must provide support and encourage them. Whenever the situation calls for it, we need to show loving discipline to our children while allowing them to grow. God does not allow us to get away with sin because if He did, how would we learn to grow in Him? It would make God look like an irresponsible father wouldn't it? Simply put, discipline is a form of love and it is sometimes needed to bring us back to Him.

Although God does not always shield us from the consequences of our decisions, He does forgive us when we ask and God will protect His people from dangers that are seen in the physical and also the dangers that are unseen in the spiritual. God provides protection on the road while driving or crossing the street, He provides protection while flying in airplanes, and even through the everyday activities in life involving our spouses and children. In the spiritual world, God does so much that we often do not see or even know is happening and as the ageless and perfect father that He is, God keeps us from the insidious and sinister plans that the devil has planned for each and every person on this earth. As discussed before, a father is to protect his children to the very end even if it costs him his life. We must give thanks to the Lord that He makes the decision to protect us even when we don't deserve it. His goodness, mercy, and faithfulness never end and He protects us because He loves us.

THE LORD DISCIPLINES THOSE WHO HE LOVES AND HE CALLS HIS CHILDREN.

PROV. 3:12, HEB. 12:6

To make this point a bit clearer, just think of the world and what it would look like if God were to remove His protection from humanity. If God were to remove His protective hand from humanity, I truly believe, it would cease to exist. Death would permeate every aspect of life. The devil would throw a ball. Thankfully, God makes sure that the enemy is kept at bay for the sake of our well-being and all of us need to do the same for the sake of our children. I am sometimes reminded of when I would hear some parents remind their children to say their prayers before bedtime. I didn't used to think much about it but now I find myself thinking of how we ask the Father for protection even at a young age. We may not do it as much as we get older but it shows that we realize our dependence on God and recognize Him as a protector. Let us realize God's decision to keep us safe and give him thanks for each breath that we take.

Part Five: The True Heart of the Father

PROVIDER AND GUIDE

—

As a father, God exhibits every characteristic a father needs to have in order to be successful. We have discussed that God is a loving and sacrificial Father who looks after each one of His children. God is also a provider who makes sure that His children have everything that they need. This is confirmed in Philippians 4:19, "And my God **shall supply all your need** according to His riches in glory by Christ Jesus." Please note the key word used in this verse is need not want. God does not want His children to be spoiled and forget that all blessings come from His gracious hand. God also does not want His blessings, though bountiful, to be taken for granted. In His infinite wisdom and love for us, God hears our requests and decides on a yes, no, or not now response. For example, if a ten-year old child were to ask his father for a real motorcycle, a good father would say, "no" or "not now" for safety (and legal) reasons but if the child were to be older, say twenties, and ask his father for a motorcycle, the father's response might be different based on the child's maturity level and the father's view on motorcycle safety.

In the same way when it comes to everyday decisions, God will provide in accordance with what is best for our lives and if something is not good for us, His answer will be no. This answer is not to disappoint, hurt, or anger us but to keep us from something potentially dangerous or harmful down the line. It is important to remember that God is a God of the small details and the big picture and when He gets involved in the intricacies of our lives, He knows what He is doing in the long run—creating a masterpiece.

WHEN WE ARE IN GOD'S WILL, HE WILL ALWAYS GIVE US WHAT WE NEED BUT NOT EVERYTHING THAT WE WANT. HE WILL NOT ENABLE US TO CREATE IDOLS. NOTHING CAN BE ALLOWED TO TAKE HIS PLACE AS NUMBER ONE IN OUR LIVES.

God will always provide for the needs of His children and sometimes, as the good father that He is, God will provide our wants. However, it is important to note that God is who He is and we are His creation created for the purpose of bringing Him glory. Whenever God gives us things that take His place as the number one thing in our lives, we have then idolized that thing or person and that is something that God will never endorse. As a result, God will not give us things that He knows will take center stage in our lives. The creator must never be replaced by the creation and when we allow idols into our lives that is what we do to God. There are even times when God will take things and people away from us. His goal is for our attention to be redirected unto Him.

In today's world, an example of this would be similar to that of a child when they receive a new computer. In a blink of an eye, their attention can be glued to the screen rather than our words, their responsibilities, and purpose. Consequently, their relationship with you takes a back seat (those with teens especially can relate to this I am sure) because all of a sudden, the gift has become much more important than the giver of the gift. As they spend all their time on this computer, your relationship with your child begins to deteriorate and you and your child slowly start to drift apart. Why? Because your relationship's priority has shifted in the child's mind and whether it is done consciously or unconsciously it hurts to take a back seat to something else. As a result, in love, corrective actions may need to be taken.

BE A SOURCE OF BLESSING AND ENCOURAGEMENT TO YOUR CHILDREN IN EVERY SEASON OF THEIR LIVES.

Our relationships with God can go in the same direction and God does not want that for us. He loves us and He wants to be in regular and constant communication with us. Jesus set that example throughout the Gospels. Jesus would go off by Himself to pray and to spend alone time with the Father, regardless of his busy schedule. Jesus knew how important it was to have a relationship with the Father. Even in the Garden of Gethsemane amidst his anguish of the suffering to come, Jesus reached out to the Father. His focus was on God and God's focus was on His Son. On the cross as Jesus bled and died for our sin, He still called out to the Father. Without a doubt, His focus was unbroken.

He made sure His relationship with the Father was not tarnished and He did what He was asked. Fathers, in the same way, our children should want to have a relationship with us. Relationships are not always easy but good ones are worth working through and each father should work to have a relationship with their children and children should see a relationship with their father as something to strive for even when things get hard or complicated. Do not discourage your children but let them see that in all things you will bless them in the way that leads to their good development.

As we discuss the Father as a provider, it is important to keep in mind that not all provision is material. God provides intangible things that we are able to enjoy every day, even some things we my not desire or things we take for granted. Examples could include our abilities to function on a daily basis, experiencing the seasons of the year that allow u to enjoy everything from a barbeque in the summer to building snowmen in the winter. God provides friends and the capacity to laugh, cry, and reach out to Him through prayer whenever we need to. While we cannot give these particular things to our children, we can share these times with them and provide them with another intangible- lifetime memories that they will cherish.

As I am writing this section and throughout this book, I have been encouraged to look at myself. What am I doing right? What do I need to improve? As I look at the qualities of God the Father, I can only look to thank Him for who He is and what He does for me each and every day. I can only look to want to be like Him with the children that He has given me but at the same time I see how far away I am and how much I need His help to do what I need to do. You cannot leave a godly legacy without God and while I am not perfect, I can strive to be godlier as I raise my children and so can each and every one of you. Oftentimes, our children will look up to us and want to be like us, so we should be diligent to do the best that we can not to let them down.

God also looks to guide us through the journey of life through His Word. Some people however, look at God's Word and see it as nothing more than a laundry list of rules and a catalog of do's and don'ts and in all of it the loving fatherhood of God is forgotten. One thing that is dismissed or misunderstood however is that much of the 'freedom' that the world shows has a price to pay in the end. All the partying, indiscriminate sex, drug use, overeating, and the like, is unfulfilling. Momentarily it may suppress certain emotions and or thoughts, but the void always returns. Only God can fill it. God's plan is to guide us into righteous living to ensure that each and every one of us escapes the clutches and snares of sinful living, repents of wrongdoing, and lives a fulfilled life.

As discussed in earlier chapters, a father's duty is to guide his children and this is one way that God as a father does this. He sets up barriers to keep each of us from falling off the edge although sometimes we try to climb over those barriers to get what we want. Even when we succeed in climbing those barriers and we fall—God is in the business of restoration. His legacy is cemented in grace and He shows us that grace each and every day. The Bible states in Romans 5:8 that, "While we were still sinners (enemies of God), Christ died for the ungodly" and as an added bonus, in Matthew 28:20 and Hebrews 13:6, Jesus made the promise to never leave us or forsake us. There are times when it seems like He is nowhere to be found but trust me, He is true to His word. God's guidance is like a GPS so even when we miss our way, His guidance will 'recalculate' to get us back on track towards His plan for us.

He created us, He knows us, and He will work with us to achieve our purpose but only if we will with work Him as well because He will not impose Himself on us.

This is one of many areas where God calls us to have faith and trust Him. He sees the big picture and looks to spare us from the danger that lurks ahead although He will not keep us from doing what we want if we persist. In life, sometimes, the best teacher is experienced and no father can shield his children from making mistakes but as in the parable of the Prodigal Son, God waits for His children to come home. He wants each one of us to learn from our mistakes and become better and not bitter by the experiences we face although in some cases, if we are being honest with ourselves, that is not what happens. God's duty is to protect and guide His children and He does but only if we allow him to. We should look to remain in the Father's hands and remember that his fences and barriers aren't to keep us away from fun but to keep harm, pain, and death away from us. We must make sure to trust in God as the holy and good father that He is.

The fact that God guides His children and establishes statutes to keep us safe is evidence of the fact that God is an ever-present father who, as King David eloquently noted in Psalm 46:1, is "God is our refuge and strength, a very present help in trouble" (ESV). In order to be a very present help, God has to be present. In times like this, we are encouraged to remember that Jesus promised to be there for us. We must cling to Him through all the trying times we may face and now that He will not fail us.

There is no debate that we live in a world that harbors, festers, and breeds evil as the devil looks to undermine God's plan and destroy God's children. In the times when God seems distant that we often tend to feel the effects (and sometimes the enticement) of this evil world around us but we are encouraged to make sure that we do not fall into it. It is then that we need to be especially sensitive to the words of the scripture and use it as our guide to light our path while combating the words of the enemy who looks to accuse and discourage us from chasing after a relationship with God. As a father, it is very important that the children know that you are always going to be there for them. Regardless of where your children may be at any given time in their life, your presence as a father must be as consistent as possible. Whether they're in boarding school, a dorm, deployment, or have a career in another town, state, or country, your role as a father still matters!

FATHERHOOD IS UNIVERSAL BECAUSE GOD IS UNIVERSAL.

The call to fatherhood is universal because God is universal. Regardless of race, financial status, physical appearance, all of us are called to leave a legacy and we will leave one whether we want to or not. Throughout this book we have had the opportunity to see that fathers have a place and are needed regardless of what Hollywood and society may say and regardless of our flaws. The key is to keep going and keep progressing. Children, whether they will admit it or not, want their fathers around and those who happen to grow up without one oftentimes will acknowledge that there is no substitute. There are times in which a father may justifiably be out of the home due to circumstances beyond his control but for others, it is due to irresponsible living, abandonment or legal issues. Whatever the circumstance, a father will leave a legacy.

He will stand before God and give an account for his role as a father. This cannot be stressed enough because on that day, excuses will not be accepted.

For the fathers who are in the home, we need to make sure that the legacy we leave is one that we and future generations can be proud of. This means that we need to look honestly at ourselves on a regular basis and be honest with our performances as fathers with the determination to improve. The main thing is to be as absolutely honest with yourself or there is no point. You can start with the following questions or come up with some of your own. Are you irresponsible? Living carelessly or selfishly, leaving damage in your wake? Are you absent? Never around for your family because you are busy building your own kingdom? Are you domineering or abusive? Do you cause your children to fear you or are you unavailable when they need you? Are you none of those things but you are passively in their lives? Are you invisible in their lives? Are there any other areas that you can see yourself not living up to your calling? What are you going to do about it or is the status quo okay for you?
I understand that life can get crazy sometimes but our children need us and we need to hold ourselves accountable for our development and theirs as well.

When we are genuine in being better fathers, we will look to fulfill our duties and responsibilities even if we struggle in areas. When we look to provide, protect, and guide, we are doing what we are called to do. When we nurture our children into successful, gracious, and humble people, we are leaving a godly legacy behind us. In order to do that however we need to be available, patient, and honest with them in the same way that God is with us time and time again. We need to spend time with them as God wants us to spend time with Him. This inevitably will lead to achieving that which we strive for—the true heart of the Father.

God is holy and He calls us to be holy because He wants us to be like Him, as we see in the life of Jesus. Throughout the Gospels, we see Jesus set the perfect example. Because of Jesus, we can come to the Father confidently and unashamed. We must emulate the sacrifice of God who made himself available and gave His best so that we can be blessed. The Father lovingly gives to those who ask, He provides, He protects, and He guides us towards better living. Even when we disobey and go our own way, He still loves us and wants longingly for us to come back to Him. We too can be fathers who do the same for our children and we have to do whatever we can to strive to achieve this standard. In case you missed it, God loves us and we are to love our children likewise.

For those who may not have a father or for those who may feel like you have blown it as a father for whatever reason, know this and believe it with all your heart: God will not abandon you. In Psalm 68:5, the scripture reminds us of one of God's amazing attributes when it describes God as, "Father of the fatherless and protector of widows is God in his holy habitation" (ESV). God is no respecter of person and does not forget those who are victims of absentee or substandard (or even evil) fathering. No man is perfect but there is a God who is, who chooses to look after those who call out to Him with a genuine heart. He is ever-present and will never leave or forsake us even when it feels like He is not there. It is His way to build us up in order for us to learn to walk by faith and not by emotion or feeling. Do not doubt His love for you. He is God, He is a father, and He is always there. Always.

REVIEW & ANALYSIS

—

Take some time to review this section. Whether you are by yourself or in a group, be honest with yourself about the following questions:

- What is your honest opinion of God being described as a father?
- Do you see God as a father? Why or why not?
- After all that we have read, what do you think God's legacy is to us?
- Are there any specific attributes of God the Father that you may want to implement as you raise your children? Why?
- How do you think you can look to emulate God's fatherly attributes as you raise your own children?

REFERENCES

(n.d.). Retrieved from Dictionary.com: http://www.dictionary.com/browse/father?s=t

Kennedy, G. J. (2015, May 7). How Loneliness Affects the Mind and Body. Retrieved from The Doctor's Tablet: http://blogs.einstein.yu.edu/how-loneliness-affects-the-mind-and-body/

Tracy, N. (2016, May 26). Emotional Abuse: Definitions, Signs, Symptoms, Examples. Retrieved from Healthy Place for Your Mental Health: https://www.healthyplace.com/abuse/emotional-psychological-abuse/emotional-abuse-definitions-signs-symptoms-examples

White Fields Community Church. (2016, June 20). The Impact on Kids of Dad's Faith and Church Attendance. Retrieved from The Longmont Pastor: https://nickcady.org/2016/06/20/the-impact-on-kids-of-dads-faith-and-church-attendance/

www.ingramcontent.com/pod-product-compliance
Lightning Source LLC
LaVergne TN
LVHW051600070426
835507LV00021B/2678